M. B. IZARD
Professor Emeritus and Consultant

ACHIEVE

consulting inc.

Lenexa, Kansas 66216
mbizard@kc.rr.com
913-268-6873

Opportunity Analysis, Business Ideas: Identification and Evaluation
Revised 2008, Copyright© 2004.

Mary Beth Izard
913-268-6873
913-522-6184
mbizard@kc.rr.com

To order contact:
Fulfillment Plus
P.O.B. 12444
North Kansas City, MO 64116
816-221-4700
e-mail: workbook@fulfillment-kc.com

ISBN 0-9728748-2-8

Opportunity Analysis
Business Ideas: Identification and Evaluation

a practical guide to identifying and evaluating ideas for a business

The gateway to entrepreneurship is a viable business idea that fits you, your talents and skills, your dreams and goals, and the marketplace. Take the first step toward starting your own business by:

- Finding out how other entrepreneurs came up with ideas for their businesses.
- Following a guided process toward discovering a viable idea.
- Identifying the next steps to becoming an entrepreneur and begin your journey.

Why this book was written_____

After years of teaching college students and adults the business planning process and how to write a business plan, it became apparent that individuals could save much time and energy by expending more effort on the front end—identifying and evaluating potential business ideas prior to writing a business plan or starting a business. Many times the ideas that individuals have do not fit their goals and dreams or do not utilize their skills. The market viability of their idea is often an afterthought.

When these facts become apparent to individuals as they write their business plans, often they lose interest and even abandon the process. How much more meaningful would it be if individuals BEGAN the process with a well thought out idea that had been validated through basic research?

The purpose of this book is to fill that gap and assist individuals in both identifying and evaluating business ideas prior to preparing of a business plan and beginning their entrepreneurial journey.

About the Author

Mary Beth Izard was a professor of entrepreneurship and marketing for 25 years. She launched the Entrepreneurship Program at Johnson County Community College in 1990 and has won numerous awards for teaching excellence. She currently teaches the course *Planning the Entrepreneurial Venture* as a Professor Emeritus.

Mary Beth was a scholar-in-residence at the Ewing Marion Kauffman Foundation from 1995-97 and has consulted on many projects since, including the blended learning course, *Planning the Entrepreneurial Venture,* and the *FastTrac® NewVenture*™ and *FastTrac® Growth Planning*™ courses. She consulted with the University of Kansas on the development of the KU Senior Academy and works with community colleges to develop entrepreneurship curricula.

An entrepreneur herself, Mary Beth has been involved in various ventures, including manufacturing, property management, and consulting.

Acknowledgments

I am most appreciative of my peers and colleagues who have supported my entrepreneurial interest over the years. A special thanks goes to Barbara Phipps, who gave me the opportunity to develop and launch an entrepreneurship program at Johnson County Community College when entrepreneurship education was just beginning to make its way into mainstream academia. My friends and colleagues at the Ewing Marion Kauffman Foundation provided feedback and suggestions for this work, particularly Beverly White and Carol Allen. I would also like to acknowledge and thank Kathy Nadlman, friend and colleague, and Melody Kamerer, professor at Butler County Community College, for their contributions. And of course, thank you and love to my biggest supporters, Brooke and Blair, my daughters, and my husband, Jack Kelsh.

I would also like to thank the hundreds of present and future entrepreneurs I have met over the years who have made my work both exciting and rewarding.

Table of Contents_____

Sources of Ideas for a Business

How many times have you talked with someone who said: "I'd love to start my own business. I just don't know what type of business to start"? Perhaps you have said this yourself. There are hundreds of books on the shelves of major retail bookstores on how to start a business and write a winning business plan. Without a business idea, however, there is no business to start or plan to write.

In order to join the 10.1 million individuals (reported by the Ewing Marion Kauffman Foundation in its publication, *The Entrepreneur Next Door)* who are actively engaged in starting new businesses in the United States, you need an idea for a business—one that fits you and will lead you to accomplish your personal, professional, and financial goals.

In this book, you will use a step-by-step approach to discovering a business idea that is right for you. You will follow the path used by other successful entrepreneurs to identify their business ideas. The path to finding the key to your future, as shown in Diagram 1.1, begins with **YOU** and is based on a two-stage process—**idea identification and idea evaluation**.

Idea Identification—Steps 1 and 2

To come up with new business idea(s) or add to the ones you already have.

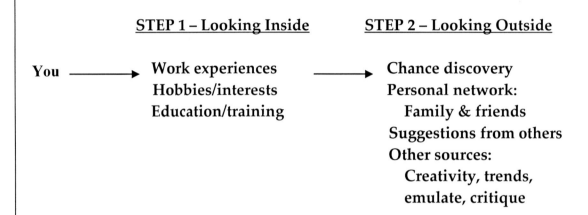

STEP 1 – Looking Inside

STEP 2 – Looking Outside

You ⟶ Work experiences
Hobbies/interests
Education/training

⟶ Chance discovery
Personal network:
    Family & friends
Suggestions from others
Other sources:
    Creativity, trends,
    emulate, critique

Idea Evaluation—Steps 3 and 4

To evaluate your business ideas and identify the one that fits you best.

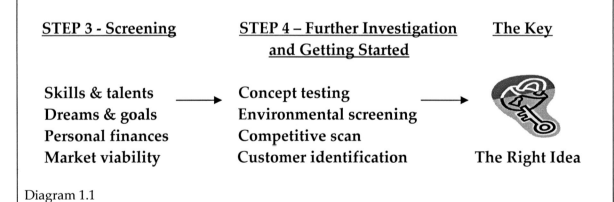

STEP 3 - Screening

STEP 4 – Further Investigation and Getting Started

The Key

Skills & talents
Dreams & goals
Personal finances
Market viability

⟶ Concept testing
Environmental screening
Competitive scan
Customer identification

⟶

The Right Idea

Diagram 1.1

In Steps 1 and 2 you complete activities in which you identify your strengths, search the marketplace for trends and unmet needs, brainstorm ideas, and synthesize information in new and different ways. These hands-on activities are essential to your idea exploration.

In Steps 3 and 4, you conduct basic market research to gain additional information on the ideas you identified in Steps 1 and 2 and determine which idea would be best to pursue. Through this process you move from the idea stage to the business concept stage. A business concept includes not only the idea for a business but clarity regarding who the targeted customers are and how they can be reached. Writing a business plan for the concept you have identified is the next logical step after you complete the activities in this book.

SOURCES OF IDEAS

Ideas for businesses come from a multitude of sources, as shown in Diagram 1.2. At the top of the list is work experience. More than any other entry strategy, entrepreneurs cite work experience as the avenue used to launch their own businesses. Through their work, many nascent entrepreneurs are able to develop skills they subsequently use in their own businesses. Some are able to identify needs and gaps in the marketplace that their current employer is not addressing and that represent an opportunity for them to start a business.

Younger people with limited work experience or people who have been out of the workforce for some time will need to focus on sources other than work for a business idea. This may include evaluating education and hobbies, examining marketplace needs, or conferring with friends and relatives. Such was the case with Rhonda, who had not worked in several years and decided that working for herself would be much more appealing than going to work for someone else. At her brother's suggestion, that others would appreciate her gardening and landscaping training and talents, she opened her own landscaping business.

In exploring ideas, its important to keep in mind that not just any idea will do. What idea can you become passionate about? Although money is a factor in assessing ideas for businesses, it should not be the determining factor; instead it should be the by-product of a business about which you are passionate. This passion can sustain you through the many challenges of business ownership.

Do what you love and the money will follow.
Author Unknown

If it is best to open a business about something you are passionate, what is your passion? What captivates you? Makes you excited about getting up in the morning? What would you like to do even if you weren't getting paid for it? For some, especially those who have not had the opportunity to try different things and explore their interests and talents, identifying a passion is its own challenge. Working through the exercises in this book will help you uncover or clarify what you enjoy and do well. You will examine all the sources of ideas identified below.

Sources of Ideas
Prior work experience
Personal interest and hobby
Chance happening
Family, relatives, and friends
Suggestion from others
Education/courses
Other

Source: Data developed and provided by the National Federation of Independent Business Foundation

Diagram 1.2

MARKET CONTEXT

An individual's search for an idea must be undertaken in the larger context of the marketplace as a whole. What entrepreneur would not be successful if he or she were able to look into the crystal ball of the future and see what products customers would buy and what industries would flourish. Without such mystical insights, however, entrepreneurs are confined to less glamorous approaches—like analyzing trends, studying the economy, and becoming careful observers of human behavior.

Rapid changes in technology today with their corresponding disruption, renovation, and transformation of the marketplace exemplify the theory of "creative destruction" espoused by Joseph Shumpeter, one of the most influential economists of the 20th century. He observed that the same innovation that creates opportunity for one business destroys another. Schumpeter cited many examples of how fledgling ventures were able to take advantage of creative destruction. Mass production in factories all but eliminated local dress and shoe shops, and the car replaced the horse and buggy. Entrepreneur.com recently cited record stores, camera film manufacturing, and pay phones on their list of businesses facing extinction in the next ten years. What technological changes caused these declines? What entrepreneurial opportunities exist today because of creative destruction rendered by innovations such as computers, the Internet, and global positioning systems?

More recently, author and forecaster Harry Dent, writes of the cyclical nature of the economy in his book, *The Next Generation Bubble Boom,* citing bubbles (booms and busts) in stocks, technology, and housing and other sectors like oil markets. He identifies the source of these bubbles as the baby boom generation with its massive purchasing power and the impact of radical new technologies and business models moving in to the mainstream. Dent writes that the bubble boom will be over in North America and most of the Western world when new technologies have penetrated around 90% of households by around late 2009 and when the massive baby-boom generation finishes its spending cycle, around 2010. Whether or not one agrees, Dent's work alerts us to the volatility of the marketplace. The good news is that opportunities exist for entrepreneurs in both boom and bust markets.

ENTREPRENEUR

The word "entrepreneur" is commonly used to describe individuals who start and run both small and large businesses. Although there is no commonly accepted delineation between a small business owner and an entrepreneur, the growth aspirations the business owner has for his or her business are what typically differentiates the two. Entrepreneurs create organizations that create jobs for others; small business owners create jobs for themselves and a small number of others—often family members.

Many individuals start out to be small business owners, but then raise their aspirations as they learn the ropes of entrepreneurship and their business meets with success.

"There are two kinds of businesses, small businesses and previously small businesses."
Author Unknown

In this book, the term "entrepreneur" is used to reference any individual who identifies a business opportunity, gathers the resources, and assumes the financial, emotional, and personal risks of launching and growing a business. The entrepreneurial examples included in this book focus on activities undertaken during the opportunity recognition and evaluation stage of the entrepreneurial process. The entrepreneurs featured in "Snapshots" throughout the book are identified by name. In the examples and the "Clips" sections of the book, names of individuals have been changed.

Theories on what drives an entrepreneur have been around for decades. Renowned economist Joseph Shumpeter, as cited in Inc. Magazine, was one of the first to venture into the unchartered waters of the entrepreneurial psyche in his book, *The Theory of Economic Development*. Shumpeter is quoted as saying that entrepreneurs feel "the will to conquer: the impulse to fight, to prove oneself superior to others, to succeed for the sake, not of the fruits of success, but of success itself …There is the joy of creating, of getting things done, or simply of exercising one's energy and ingenuity."

Although there is no one set of skills and characteristics of successful entrepreneurs, ones commonly cited include marketplace sensitivity, networking, effective communications, calculated risk taking, perseverance, and high-achievement needs. In the entrepreneurs featured throughout the book, note how they demonstrated these characteristics in pursuing their entrepreneurial dreams.

Successful entrepreneurs learn to fail quickly and cheaply.
Author Unknown

YOUR COMPETITIVE ADVANTAGE

A competitive advantage sets you and your business apart from others in the marketplace. It may stem from skills and talents you possess that are unique or hard to find. It may be based on your ability to offer a product or service in a creative, innovative way, perhaps to a niche market.

As you proceed with the activities in Step 1, looking within yourself for an idea for a business, think about what you do best. All people possess characteristics that make them special or different, and define their place within the family, peer group, school or work environment. These same characteristics may allow them to define a unique space in the marketplace and be the source of their competitive advantage. This was the case with Isabella, an interior designer, whose talents as an artist allowed her to provide sketches and renderings of decorating projects of a quality unmatched by her colleagues. Ethan, a very sociable young man, was able to launch a successful real estate business as a result of his knack for connecting with people and his ability to build relationships quickly. Both of these entrepreneurs started businesses that capitalized on the personal skills and talents they possessed and provided them a competitive advantage.

What do you do well? What have others told you that you excel at? What have you received recognition for in the past? What innate talents do you possess that perhaps you never had the opportunity to express or develop? These talents and aptitudes may be the source of **your** future competitive advantage.

According to Farrah Gray, a 22-year entrepreneur who made his first million dollars at age 15 and the author of the book, *Reallionaire, Nine Steps to Becoming Rich from the Inside Out*, successful entrepreneurship stems from defining your area of excellence. He suggests that potential entrepreneurs ask themselves the following questions to identify their passion and an idea for a business:
- What comes easy for me and hard for others?
- What work would I do even if I weren't getting paid?
- What can I give back?

The more you know about the marketplace in which you plan to operate, the more capable you will be of creating or identifying your competitive advantage. It's important to remember, however, that it is not the idea that leads to success, but the perseverance to follow your dreams and the ability to implement your plan with excellence.

"opportunity is missed by most people because it is dressed in overalls and looks like work."

Thomas Edison

Step 1

Looking Internally for Business Ideas

Step 1 Objective

To identify possible business ideas through:

- Analyzing current and previous work experiences.

- Examining personal hobbies and interests.

- Evaluating education and skills.

Prior and Present Work Experiences

Work experience is the No. 1 source of ideas for starting a business. Some entrepreneurs capitalize on what they learned working for others and either copy or slightly modify products or services their previous or current employer offers in the marketplace. Others offer products or services similar to what their employer offers but to different target markets, often focusing on small or underserved market niches that their employer does not pursue. This latter strategy fits both the budget and the competitive abilities of a new business. For example, an entrepreneur in Hawaii started a successful small business making custom shirts for corporations and sports teams. Her previous employer, a producer of Hawaiian-style shirts, did not serve this market niche because it took too much time away from his core business, Hawaiian shirts.

Starting a new venture requires a significant amount of learning. If you can begin your entrepreneurial journey armed with technical and industry knowledge acquired on a previous job, your business launch and early growth will go much more smoothly and you will greatly reduce the number of mistakes you will likely make. Yes, we all make mistakes in the process of learning. As one entrepreneur put it, "Learn on someone else's checkbook."

self check

To help you identify entrepreneurial opportunities that build on your previous work and industry experiences, ask yourself:

- Do customers complain of a problem that my employer does not address?

- Can I save customers money by doing things slightly differently than my employer?
- Can I develop a product or service to complement those offered by my employer?
- What other markets—those not currently being reached—exist for my employers' products or services?
- Is the market growing at such a rate that it offers an opportunity for new entrants into the field?

Although identifying an idea for a business while working for someone else is common, many would-be entrepreneurs struggle with giving up the security of a corporate job and assuming the risks of entrepreneurship. At first glance, the risks may seem great. Upon closer scrutiny, however, the risks associated with depending on someone else for one's livelihood prompts many to take the entrepreneurial leap. This is particularly true in today's volatile economic environment. Nascent entrepreneurs frequently see a greater security in depending upon themselves and their own skills and abilities to generate an income than on an employer. The financial security they feel they will realize, coupled with the desirability of being one's own boss—the reason entrepreneurs most frequently give for starting their own businesses—often tips the scale toward entrepreneurship.

self check

Compare the advantages and disadvantages of being an employee and an entrepreneur by answering the following questions:

Employee	Entrepreneur
1. What are financial benefits?	1. What are the financial benefits?
2. What are the short and long-term financial risks?	2. What are the short and long-term financial risks?
3. What are the emotional rewards?	3. What are the emotional rewards?
4. What are the emotional risks?	4. What are the emotional risks?

Only you can access whether or not the benefits of pursuing an entrepreneurial future outweigh the risks.

"Information is the key to overcoming fear."
Author Unknown

Clips

- Abigail left her job as a graphic designer to start her own graphic design company.
- Hector started his own remodeling company after years of working for someone else.
- Carol left her job with a major advertising and public relations firm to start her own public relations firm.

LADDERING

When you work for someone else, not only do you learn a job, you also learn an industry. Laddering refers to the concept of broadening your search for business ideas beyond your current or previous job by considering possibilities at different levels within your industry's distribution ladder.

Laddering Vertically

Each link in the distribution ladder—producing, selling, transporting, and packaging the product along the path from producer to customer—adds value in some way. Activity 1.2 encourages you to look at the entire distribution system for your industry, where you fit into it, and what other opportunities may exist as a result of your industry knowledge and experience. The consumer and business products distribution ladders typically have multiple levels, as shown in Diagram 1.3. The service distribution ladder is much shorter, as often the producer (service provider) works directly with the customer. There may be no intermediary steps.

In some industries, the distribution ladder may be more condensed than shown, as one level within the ladder performs the functions of the levels above and/or below. The Internet has dramatically altered the way some products are distributed, flattening the distribution process and creating exciting opportunities for astute entrepreneurs. Many entrepreneurs are now able to offer their products directly to customers through the Internet.

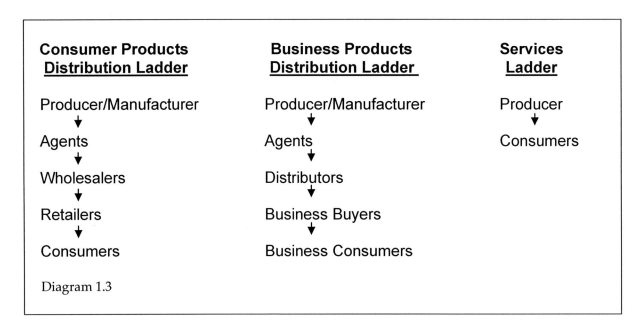

Consumer Products Distribution Ladder	Business Products Distribution Ladder	Services Ladder
Producer/Manufacturer	Producer/Manufacturer	Producer
↓	↓	↓
Agents	Agents	Consumers
↓	↓	
Wholesalers	Distributors	
↓	↓	
Retailers	Business Buyers	
↓	↓	
Consumers	Business Consumers	

Diagram 1.3

Following are several examples of how moving from one rung to another on the distribution ladder provided a worker an opportunity to become an entrepreneur.

Example Consumer Products Distribution Ladder

A store manager moved up the consumer products distribution ladder to become a manufacturer's representative and sell the products he previously purchased. This person's knowledge of the products and industry enabled him to start his own business and move from the retail to the wholesale level.

Example Business Products Distribution Ladder

A teacher started her own business selling educational materials to school districts and other teachers as an independent sales representative for a publisher of textbooks, test materials, and reading programs. She moved from being a consumer on the business products distribution ladder to the agent level. As a teacher, she had used a variety of educational products that were sold to her school district. Her knowledge of these products and the distribution system enabled her to make this transition.

In her search for a business idea, she considered, but did not pursue writing, publishing, and marketing her own educational materials.

Example **Services Distribution Ladder**

The research director in charge of drug testing for a large pharmaceutical company started her own pharmaceutical consulting and drug testing company. Her first client was her former employer. Contracting services back to former employers can be an excellent business entry strategy, as employers may be happy to subcontract work to former employees who are competent and left on good terms.

In another instance, an information technology (IT) manager for a large company hired many IT consultants to augment his company's in-house IT work force. This experience helped him identify the opportunity of starting his own IT consulting firm, providing IT staff to companies such as the one for which he worked, thus moving up the services distribution ladder from being a consumer of services to that of providing services. You will read more about this entrepreneur in the Snapshot that follows.

Snapshot of Entrepreneur

As a director of global network engineering for a large company, Robert Jewell was frequently in need of talented IT staff. The demand for such skills far outstripped the supply of qualified consultants. As a result Robert started his own business, Network Integration Services (NIS), an IT consulting firm specializing in the design and deployment of information technology services. Starting primarily in networking, workstations, and servers, NIS later added expertise in electrical engineering, disaster recovery planning, and high availability computing environments. Robert's previous employer was one of his early clients.

By addressing the need for highly skilled labor, Robert has continued to grow his company successfully. He enrolled in the FastTrac™ Growth Planning course, developed by the Ewing Marion Kauffman Foundation, to assist him in developing a growth strategy for the company. In an industry in which anyone could hang up a shingle, NIS added a level of professionalism by touting its engineering background and focusing on quality.

Snapshot of Entrepreneur

Diane James noticed that many of her aging baby boomer friends and acquaintances were having serious concerns about long-term care expenses for their aging parents as well as themselves down the road. Some lacked financial resources to fund nursing home care. Those who had the resources hated seeing their life savings go toward paying nursing home expenses. Diane saw their concerns as a business opportunity.

Her discussions with several financial planners confirmed the need for baby boomers to begin to plan for long-term health care for their later years.

Establishing an insurance agency to sell long-term care insurance to the consumer market, Diane capitalized on her prior work experience as vice president of marketing for a health insurance company. Her new company, the James Agency, sold different products from those of her previous employer and her marketing expertise allowed her to move from the corporate world to owning her own business and having more control over her time and resources. Her former employer referred inquiries for long-term care to Diane.

Could you be a successful entrepreneur like Diane by leveraging your work experience into a new business opportunity?

Laddering Horizontally

This refers to starting a business by using your work experience and skills in an industry other than the one in which you work. Skills such as planning, organizing, leading, controlling, project managing, and marketing are readily transferable from one situation to another. Many who have these skills have a great deal of mobility. Often technical skills are transferable as well. This was the case of the medical doctor who acted as a consultant to attorneys in medical malpractice cases and a police officer who consulted on security-related issues to small businesses. Are there other industries in which you could use your skills and talents?

Clips

- Carey, a computer analyst, started his own computer security consulting firm.

- Chen, an accountant, started a skip-tracing business to track down individuals who did not pay their bills and had legal judgments against them. As an accountant in a small company, he often had to find such individuals, thereby learning how to do so.

- Carmina, a college professor teaching management, utilized her considerable teaching experience to develop seminars for a corporate training company.

 **activity
1.1 360-degree perspective of ME,
present and previous work
experiences**

My work experiences

a. My current or most recent job — responsibilities, duties, and activities

b. Skills/talents used in my current or most recent job

c. My previous jobs — responsibilities, duties, and activities

d. Skills/talents used in my previous jobs

e. I am an expert on

f. Ideas that relate to unmet market needs or niche markets observed through current or previous work experiences

g. Brainstorm business ideas that relate to present and previous jobs and areas of expertise. Do not evaluate how feasible or desirable these ideas are at this time.

Synthesis of past and present work experiences

Of the many ideas you listed above, which ones appeal to you the most and why?

1.2 activity
laddering – present and previous work experiences

Laddering

a. **Circle distribution ladder heading**. In your current or most recent job, did you provide a consumer product, a business product, or a service? Circle the appropriate heading below. *(If your job involves more than one distribution ladder [for example, your company provides both a product and a service] you may wish to examine each separately by completing this activity for each.)*

Consumer Products Distribution Ladder	Business Products Distribution Ladder	Services Ladder
Producer/Manufacturer ↓	Producer/Manufacturer ↓	Producer ↓
Agents ↓	Agents ↓	Consumers
Wholesalers ↓	Distributors ↓	
Retailers ↓	Business Buyers ↓	
Consumers	Business Consumers	

b. **Circle rung on distribution ladder.** For the distribution ladder that you identified above, at what level did/do you work?

Vertical Laddering

c. For your current or most recent job, list individuals with whom you work(ed) closely, both inside and outside of the company.

d. Brainstorm how you can utilize your skills and experience by moving up or down your industry's distribution ladder (perhaps to the level of someone you identified under item "c" above).

e. If you started your own business, could you subcontract your skills back to your present or previous employer(s)?   _____ Yes   _____ No   _____ Not Sure
(If you are not sure, who can you contact to find out?)

Horizontal Laddering

f. What types of businesses could you start in order to provide your products or services to other industries?

Synthesis of laddering

Of the many ideas generated above, based on laddering either vertically or horizontally, which appeal to you the most and why?

Personal Hobbies and Interests

In considering potential business ideas, many nascent entrepreneurs become enthusiastic about turning a hobby or personal interest into a business. Although this entry strategy may be a good one, enthusiasm must be tempered with a realistic assessment of the commercial feasibility of such an endeavor.

The major benefit of this entry strategy is that you will be doing something you like or even love. This passion often sustains a person during the challenging early years of a business startup. Also, you have acquired experience and expertise and made contacts that will be helpful in your business.

One challenge of turning a hobby into a business is to balance the passion for the hobby aspect with the need to devote adequate time and energy to the entrepreneurial side—planning, marketing, bookkeeping, and finance.

Answer the following questions.

- Do I have an interest in turning any of my hobbies in to a business?
- If so, would I be able to produce enough to have a successful business?

Entrepreneurs are getting crafty—they are turning their crafts into successful businesses. The craft and hobby industry has experienced steady growth over the last several years, and this increase is expected to continue. The Internet has afforded thousands of crafting enthusiasts an avenue to sell their wares. For as little as $25 for a domain name and a nominal fee for a Web hosting service, an entrepreneur can open shop, so to speak. Online craft stores and eBay® are other avenues through which to sell one's wares. Thousands of discussion groups on the Internet offer support and information to those interested in hobbies from knitting to winemaking.

By closely examining your hobbies and interests and the underlying skills and talents utilized, you will gain a better understanding of your natural abilities and what you enjoy doing. Individuals are often attracted to hobbies and interests in areas in which they excel. Identifying a business idea in which you use these skills and talents can lead to success and personal fulfillment. For example, Tonya enjoyed working jigsaw puzzles in her spare time. Upon closer analysis of her hobby, she realized that working puzzles gave her an opportunity to be analytical, pay close attention to detail, and see a project through from beginning to end. After some brainstorming, she decided that starting a business as an event planner would allow her to utilize these natural abilities and preferences for detailed, project-oriented work.

Turning a hobby into a business was the avenue pursued by Clancy, a race car enthusiast that is featured in the entrepreneurial Snapshot later in the book. Clancy began his race car trailer manufacturing business part time as a way to combine work with pleasure. Through years of participating in racing activities, he was knowledgeable of the wants and needs of race car owners. He left his full-time job after orders for his trailers grew to the point where he could no longer run his business part time. Now his many hours at racing events serve a two-fold purpose: enjoying the sport and selling custom-built race car trailers.

Capitalizing on the experience they gained through personal remodeling projects and building several homes of their own, Rickeena and Chris began building homes as a sideline to other full-time jobs. They contracted out many basic home building tasks, then moved into the home and finished all the detail work, such as woodworking and painting. They lived in the home for two to three years while they completed the project and began work on their next home. Once the next home-building project was inhabitable, they would sell the home they lived in and start the process again. Upon retirement, home building became a full-time project for the couple. Although this type of enterprise is not for everyone, it allowed this couple to use their skills and talents and augment their income nicely.

It is important to consider not only the hobby itself, but everything that surrounds it. Similar to the discussion of "Laddering" in the previous section, many hobbyists identify business ideas by not only looking at their hobby but also the whole industry that supports it. If your hobby is gardening, you could start a business designing gardens and landscaping for others, teaching classes about gardening, writing books on gardening, becoming a distributor of gardening materials, or caring for floral and plant displays in corporate office buildings.

One of the caveats of turning a hobby or personal interest into a business is that your passion may become a job. Then what will you do for fun and recreation?

Snapshot of Entrepreneur

Let's hear about a successful entrepreneur who started a business based on one of her favorite hobbies—cooking:

Anna Molina loved to cook and her husband loved to fish. Living in Key Largo, they combined their interests by opening a seafood restaurant, which they ran for five years. After a divorce brought Anna back to her native Kansas City several years later, she again pursued her dream of restaurant ownership. While taking college coursework in hospitality management and entrepreneurship at a local community college, Anna spent six years looking for just the right location for her next restaurant venture.

She started El Caribe Café, a Caribbean restaurant featuring a variety of seafood and other dishes of Spanish, Cuban, Jamaican, Puerto Rican, and Brazilian origin. Catering weddings and special events also makes up a significant portion of Anna's business.

Clips

- Susan turned her quilting hobby into a quilting services and supply shop.

- Mike grew his hobby of making mission-type wood furniture into a business as a specialty furniture producer, selling through designers and retailers.

- Leslie, a nurse and gourmet cook, started a catering company aimed at customers with special dietary needs.

- Jordan's love of bicycling propelled him to start a retail bike shop specializing in equipment and clothing for cyclists.

- Tyrone's hobby of building wood chests indirectly led him to start an engraving business. After experiencing difficulty in finding someone to engrave the small brass plates he attached to the front of his wood chests, he identified an opportunity to do engraving for others. He specializes in engraving trophies and plaques for businesses and schools.

- Rachel's love of dance and years of experience led to the opening of her own dance studio.

- April, who enjoyed making gift baskets, found that her hobby "took over her life" to the point that, after three years of doing business on the side, she quit her day job. She marketed her baskets at craft fairs and in gift shops in nearby resort communities.

1.3 activity
a 360-degree perspective of ME, hobbies, interests, passions, and pastimes

My hobbies and interests

a. Things I like to do — hobbies, interests, and pastimes

b. Things I have enjoyed doing in the past

c. Things I am passionate about

d. What I like (or liked) about items listed under "c"

e. Skills and talents used in my hobbies and passions

f. Brainstorm ideas for businesses that relate to items cited above. Include ideas that could use the skills and talents you developed in the above activities. Withhold evaluation of the feasibility or desirability of ideas at this time.

Synthesis of hobbies, interests, passions, and pastimes

Of the many business ideas relating to your hobbies, interests, and pastimes, which appeal to you the most and why?

Education and Skills

Closely scrutinizing your educational background and technical skills can help you identify specific expertise that may lend itself to starting your own business. Through years in the educational system, you will have gained an understanding of where you excel.

Such was the case of Beverly, a middle-age woman who had always done well in classes that allowed her to tap her creativity and artistic interests. She returned to college to pursue an interior design degree in order to launch her own interior design business. Through an internship, which was a part of her college curriculum, she was able to build ties within the design community and further prepare herself for her eventual business ownership. Many years in the classroom may have also enabled you to develop expertise and skills that can be marketed to others in the marketplace.

"It is possible to fly without motors, but not without knowledge and skill."

Wilbur Wright

Some entrepreneurs work backwards, identifying the type of business they wish to start, and then acquiring the requisite skills and knowledge. They may enroll in college or formal certificate programs, or they may pursue informal types of training and non-credit coursework. Such was the case of Brad, a human resources director who enrolled in courses at the local

31

community college to learn more about entrepreneurship, preparing a business plan, marketing, and management in order to launch his own staffing company.

In technical fields, the skills you have today may not be the ones you need tomorrow, so education is a continual process. The need for lifelong learning is a necessity for functioning effectively on a personal level as well, whether operating the latest computer, cell phone, or PDA.

Perhaps you have taken coursework or developed your own expertise through a lengthy period of trial and error and independent learning. Or you may have had the opportunity to work closely with a talented individual who taught you the skills of a trade. There is no one way to acquire the knowledge and skills to become a successful entrepreneur. Persistence and an openness to new information and experiences will enable you to grow into the person you need to become to succeed in business.

> "The great aim of education is not
> knowledge but action."
>
> Herbert Spencer

Snapshot of Entrepreneur

Let's hear the story of an entrepreneur who started a business based on her education, coursework, skills, and interests.

Susan Davidson launched a business to provide services to accelerate the integration of foreign managers and expatriates and their families into the social and business communities of the United States.

Susan had a passion for working with the international community. On any given Saturday night, a dinner party at her home might include guests from Russia, France, Italy, or Kenya. She had traveled extensively, studying and living in a number of foreign countries. Susan studied Spanish in Guatemala and had majored in French in college.

A visit with a SCORE (Service Core of Retired Executives) counselor at the SBA (Small Business Administration), a retired international marketing executive, helped Susan develop her business idea into a workable plan. She strengthened her personal coaching skills by attending an accredited corporate coaching training program in tandem with launching her business, Beyond Borders.

Clips

- Ramon capitalized on his degree in horticulture and started his own landscaping business.

- Danielle's degree in hospitality management and training as a chef prepared her to start her own business as a personal chef.

- Bobby started a kitchen design shop utilizing her design background.

- John's training in heating and air conditioning prepared him to open his own heating and air conditioning service, which grew to employ 11 others.

- Tatiana's master's degree in botany motivated her to grow and sell orchids and other exotic plants, both wholesale and retail.

activity
a 360-degree perspective of ME, education, skills, and talents

My educational background

a. My favorite subjects in school

b. Why these subjects interested me

c. Training and skills I have acquired outside of my formal education

d. Training and skills I would like to strengthen through either formal or informal learning

What I am good at

e. What I am good at now

f. What I have been good at in the past

g. What has resulted in positive recognition and/or awards?

h. Skills and talents utilized in questions "d," "e," and "f"

i. Others would say my skills and talents are

j. Brainstorm a list of ideas for businesses that relate to your favorite subjects, strengths, and talents. Withhold evaluation of the feasibility or desirability ideas at this time.

Synthesis of education and skills

Of the many business ideas relating to your education, skills, and talents, which appeal to you the most and why?

Step 1

synthesis of ideas generated by looking internally, activities 1.1 – 1.4

Looking back over each of the activities in Step 1, list all ideas included in the **Synthesis** sections at the end of activities 1.1 - 1.4.

Step 2

Looking Externally for Business Ideas

Step 2 Objective

To identify possible business ideas through:

- Identifying needs, wants, and problems in the marketplace.

- Obtaining feedback and suggestions from others.

- Applying creative approaches to improve and change existing products or services.

- Identifying marketplace trends and related business opportunities.

Discovery by Chance

There is often a bit of serendipity in life, a coming together of luck, preparation, and hard work. This is also true in entrepreneurship. A number of entrepreneurs cite chance happenings as the source of the ideas for their businesses.

> "I'm a great believer in luck, and I find the harder I work,
> the more I have of it."
>
> Thomas Jefferson

This chance happening might take the form of listening to the off-hand comment of a co-worker or reading a certain article in a magazine or newspaper. It might be an observation of a common problem that others experience in the marketplace or a frequent irritation or frustration that you experience, such as having difficulty obtaining a particular product or service. While traveling, you might notice that certain products are available in other cities or countries that are not found at home. Or the chance happening could be a personal observation of what products and services are increasingly in demand in the marketplace. Rarely is there a shortage of ideas, just a shortage of those willing and able to implement them.

For Dan Dye and Mark Beckloff, founders of Three-Dog Bakery, now a multimillion dollar global enterprise, this chance happening occurred when a veterinarian told them that one of

39

their three rescue dogs, Gracie, needed the same kind of healthy food with no preservatives, dyes, or added fats and sugars you would feed a sick family member (The Kansas City Star). That information, along with the cookie cutter received one Christmas, spawned the original dog "cookies" that were the genesis of their dog bakery business.

You can make your own luck, or at least greatly improve it, by engaging in specific, goal-directed activities. For example, one entrepreneur recalled regularly browsing the classified ads of local and regional newspapers to identify the types of people, skills, or services being sought. He interpreted numerous ads in any one category as an indication of a potential business opportunity to provide those skills in the market.

Ideas for businesses are everywhere if you raise your antennae to pick up on them. The key is to stay alert to possibilities and to record them for further consideration. By working through the activities in this section, you can greatly improve the odds that chance happenings will afford you valuable business ideas. You will follow a structured approach for identifying and recording business possibilities gathered from observing the wants and needs of those around you, scanning magazines and newspapers, and talking with others.

"Small opportunities are often the beginning of great enterprises."

Demosthenes

Snapshot of Entrepreneur

Let's hear about a successful entrepreneur who started a business by being observant of problems both he and others experienced.

When Monte Mitchell had difficulty getting an accurate inside measurement using a traditional tape measure on a home remodeling job, he decided to do something about it. He invented and patented the Measuring Stick, with a built-in level vial, which allows the user to take precise measurements of hard-to-reach areas. His business, Accu-Measure, Inc., sells this unique measuring device through more than 100 Harbor Freight Tools stores around the country and its online catalog at www.harborfreight.com.

Monte started his company with the idea of helping people make their lives easier. He subsequently developed another product as a result of watching a tree-trimming crew cut limbs high above the ground. His product, the Professional Pole Saw, weighs only 5 pounds and has an extension of 22 feet. The Professional Pole Saw is used at numerous golf courses and theme parks around the country, including Busch Gardens.

By being observant about his needs and the needs and frustrations of others, Monte was able to come up with these winning products.

Clips

- Robert noticed an increased environmental concern regarding mold in homes and office buildings, so he took the necessary courses to become qualified to evaluate and test homes and businesses for mold.

- Upon moving to the United States, Penelope experienced difficulty obtaining food items and spices from her homeland, Bolivia. She started a retail store to provide these items to others who, like her, longed for the "taste" of home.

2.1

activity
idea log

Ideas

Keep a log of possible ideas for a product or service by observing what is going on around you. Look closely at your local community. What problems have you experienced in the marketplace? What frustrations have you observed other consumers experiencing or have you heard others talk about? What unfulfilled wants or needs do people have? What opportunities are identified in magazines or newspapers?

Idea	**Source of Idea**	**How Idea Was Identified**
Brief description of idea	Need? Want? Problem? Frustration?	Personal observation? Talking with others? Magazine? Newspaper article? (Date)

Example

In-home care for aging parents	*Need*	*Talking with others, personal observation*

Yours

1. _____ _____ _____

   _____ _____ _____

2. _____ _____ _____

   _____ _____ _____

3. _____ _____ _____

   _____ _____ _____

4. _____   _____   _____

   _____   _____   _____

5. _____   _____   _____

   _____   _____   _____

6. _____   _____   _____

   _____   _____   _____

7. _____   _____   _____

   _____   _____   _____

8. _____   _____   _____

   _____   _____   _____

Synthesis of chance discovery—"We make our own luck."

Of the many ideas noted on your Idea Log, which ones appeal to you the most and why?

Personal Network – Family and Friends

Networking is a critical skill for successful entrepreneurship. By definition, networking involves building a supportive system for sharing information and services among those having a common interest. Over the years, people typically build a network of friends and associates they can look to for ideas, information, and support.

A network may be either informal, such as a group of friends, or formal, such as a professional association. As you grow older, you may find that many of your friends are people with whom you work or conduct business. Professional contacts become personal friends.

People often underestimate the extent of their personal and professional network. It may include neighbors, friends, teachers, or the banker you have grown to know over the years. It may include those you worked with in the past, such as peers, customers, or suppliers. You may have met members of your personal network in volunteer situations, such as coaching your child's sports teams, or in professional or social groups, such as the Rotary Club or a tennis group.

Many individuals rely heavily on their informal network during the idea and business concept stage of venture creation. For example, they will discuss their desire to start a business with family members and close friends and, in many cases, use this informal network to evaluate the pros and cons of various business ideas.

Since your family and friends know you well, they can help you determine if a business idea fits your skills, talents, and interests. They can often provide insights that you do not have about your own skills and abilities. Friends know a different side of you than family members do, and they have a perspective that may give you different insights into your strengths.

You may also find that you have skills that would be of value to a family member or friend who either owns his or her own business or would be interested in starting one with you. Potential advantages of going into business with family and friends include the loyalty of members through difficult times and shared values. Stability and the ability to make long term decisions in a family business can also provide a competitive advantage in the marketplace.

Challenges include the carry over of family roles in to the workplace and the difficulties this may create. For example, the head of the household may not be the best individual to run the business. Decision making can also be challenging as emotions disrupt the process, and raising capital can be difficult.

Despite these challenges, this practice is common. Clearly defining roles and responsibilities for all positions in the company and treating relationships in a professional, business like manner can help avoid some of the pitfalls associated with partnering or employing those closest to us.

> "call it a clan, call it a network, call it a tribe,
> call it a family. whatever you call it,
> whoever you are, you need one."
>
> Jane Howard, *"Families"*

If members of your personal network are skeptical of entrepreneurship, you may not receive the support you need to pursue your entrepreneurial dream. If such is the case, you will need to broaden your network to include those more favorably disposed to or experienced in entrepreneurship, such as other entrepreneurs, business and entrepreneurship faculty, or other business people.

Once you start your business, networking becomes even more critical; and you need an expanded, more formal network to provide you guidance and support. This network might include your accountant, attorney, and banker. It might also include entrepreneurs you know and who may act as mentors. Networking will be critical to identifying and reaching potential customers as well.

In this section, you will start by looking at your personal network to identify your strengths and brainstorm possible business ideas. You will also consider your personal network to identify potential mentors in starting and growing a business.

Consider including potential mentors and key members of your network on an advisory committee for your business. Advisory committee members are strategically chosen for the knowledge and experience they can offer. An advisory committee typically meets every few months over breakfast or lunch, and members share their insights and expertise to assist the entrepreneur in guiding the business.

Snapshot of Entrepreneur

Let's hear about a successful entrepreneur who started a business utilizing the knowledge she acquired about property management from her family.

Raised around the small family real estate business, Lonah Birch became actively involved in buying real estate and managing property after the death of her mother. At that time, Lonah developed a business plan and started working her plan. With her husband and partner, she gradually acquired 22 rental units, working up to 20 hours a week, primarily on weekends and in the evening. When the 22 units were paid off, Lonah and her husband felt that they could quit their daytime jobs.

Lonah's goal was to provide clean, affordable rental property. She accomplished her goal, averaging a 95 percent occupancy rate, with several residents staying more than a decade.

Clips

- Paul and Kate, a husband and wife team, opened a farm fertilizer, feed, and supply store in their rural community. As farmers themselves, they knew the types of products farmers needed.

- Juan bought the used equipment and van from his retiring uncle to start his own guttering company.

- David joined the family plumbing business and later bought out other family members' shares.

- Brothers Alan and John started a home remodeling business. Alan was the numbers person and John was the craftsman. Together they grew a successful business.

- Richard and Tameca, co-workers and friends, started their own software development company.

- Renee and Kelly, sisters-in-law, combined their artistic training and talents and a hobby of making jewelry into a full-time business selling jewelry through a website and at local events.

- Tony began working in the family's Italian restaurant in high school and went on to later buy out other family members' interests.

2.2 activity
personal network – family and friends

My family and friends

Those closest to you are a valuable resource for possible entrepreneurial ideas and opportunities.

a. Talk to at least three close friends and members of your near and extended family. Ask them what business ideas would appropriately utilize your strengths, interests, and experiences. List their ideas below.

Name of Individual Surveyed	My Strengths	Possible Business ideas
1._____	_____	_____
	_____	_____
	_____	_____
2._____	_____	_____
	_____	_____
	_____	_____
3._____	_____	_____
	_____	_____
	_____	_____

b. From your discussions, what did you learn about others' perceptions of your strengths and abilities?

c. From your circle of family and friends, identify which individuals might become a part of your entrepreneurial support system and/or a resource for you in starting your own business.

              Name   How he or she might be helpful or supportive

1._____   _____

2._____   _____

3._____   _____

d. Which family members, relatives, and friends own their own businesses?

           Name   Type of business

_____   _____

_____   _____

_____   _____

_____   _____

_____   _____

e. Brainstorm a list of ways you could contribute to a family member's or friend's existing business. Withhold evaluation of the feasibility or desirability of doing so at this time.

Synthesis of personal network

Of the many ideas generated in this activity, which ones appeal to you the most and why?

Suggestions from Others

In the last section, you accessed your personal network of family members and friends as a source of information for identifying business ideas. Now you will consider members of your extended network for additional sources of input and support.

Consider individuals such as classmates, parents of close friends, professors, neighbors, suppliers, co-workers, and colleagues as members of your extended network. These individuals may act as personal and professional supporters and advocates. They may help you identify which of your personal skills and strengths may provide you a competitive edge in the marketplace. Or they may share with you their perception of marketplace needs.

Self check

Time yourself for one minute, and write down as many names as possible of people that are a part of your extended network.

- How many names are on your list?
- Is your network large and extensive or narrow and focused?
- What are the sources of most of the names on your list?
- Which of the individuals on your list might be a source of support or expertise for your entrepreneurial endeavors?

Remember that when you are obtaining input from others, their ideas and suggestions reflect their own personal perceptions and experiences. Your challenge is to determine whether their perceptions are shared by others. For example, Melissa came up with an idea for a business by talking with her neighbor, who expressed frustration at her inability to locally find fashionable shoes in her size, which was quite large. This person typically had to order her shoes or shop in larger cities. Although this neighbor's suggestion, opening a women's shoe store specializing in large sizes, was interesting, much research needed to be done to determine if it was a market opportunity. Were there enough women wearing large sizes to make this a profitable venture? Prior to concluding her research, Nordstrom, a large department store known for its shoe department, including large-sized ones, moved into the area. Melissa decided not to pursue the business as Nordstrom would be a formidable competitor.

Another question to consider is whether or not you have the type of network that you will need to start and grow a successful business. As you reflect on your current one, most of you will decide that you do not. If such is the case, the concept of targeted networking can help you build the network you need.

TARGETED NETWORKING

Targeted networking, in the context in which is it used in this book, is the process of identifying and nurturing relationships with individuals who can contribute to and support your success as an entrepreneur. Typically, this would include other entrepreneurs, bankers, lawyers, accountants, and key members of your industry. Your first challenge is to identify who these people are and how to meet them.

Having a mentor may also be helpful. Mentors typically share their knowledge and expertise and possibly introduce you to others who can assist you. Many individuals would like to have a mentor but are stymied by how to go about it. One way is to identify organizations or groups to which potential mentors belong and then join them. There are numerous ways to ascertain these organizations—talking with others, searching the Internet and the local Yellow Pages for trade or professional organizations, checking the Encyclopedia of Associations found at most libraries, and so on. For example, many business owners belong to their local chambers of commerce; and joining the chamber would be an excellent way of making contact.

In selecting an organization, determine if the organization's goals are consistent with yours and if the organization is a vehicle for individuals to exchange information, ideas, support, and contacts. Many organizations will allow potential members to attend several meetings prior to making a decision to join.

Another consideration is to make the most of networking opportunities in the organizations to which you already belong. Do you hold an office? Volunteer your time? Act as a speaker? Attend events where you arrive early and stay late to make the most of opportunities to meet others?

Upon meeting a person who could potentially be helpful in your entrepreneurial endeavors, a simple request to be able to contact that person in the future is typically the next step. Asking the person to meet for coffee or lunch to discuss a particular topic is a good way to begin.

Mentoring relationships develop slowly and require time and energy on the part of both parties. Like other relationships, they need to be a win-win. The reward for the mentor is often the feeling of satisfaction that comes from giving back and helping others.

Snapshot of Entrepreneur

Let's hear about a successful entrepreneur who started a business by listening to another's suggestion.

Clancy Schmidt has had many businesses over the years, including one making large trailers to transport sports cars. This business, Speedwagon Trailers, was the result of his wish to combine business and pleasure and turn his hobby, sports car racing, into a business venture.

One Sunday afternoon, a friend of Clancy's, an avid football fan, dragged him to a professional football game to show him what tailgate parties were all about. He suggested to Clancy that tailgaters needed a small, portable trailer designed to transport coolers, grills, tables, and tailgate supplies to these sporting events. To produce such trailers, Clancy and a small group of friends invested their money to launch Mobile Concepts. The original customers for this small, lightweight trailer were tailgaters, sports fans who went to games early to eat and socialize. But the prime customers ultimately became major beverage companies, which used the tailgate trailers for grocery store promotions. Clancy's friend's suggestion was the spark that ignited this venture.

Clips

- Randy decided to offer game-bird hunts on his 300-acre farm. As a result of local acquaintances' encouragement after many successful hunts, Randy began advertising these hunts regionally. Participation in hunts grew to the point that he built a separate eating facility to serve hot breakfasts and other meals to the many hunters who visited the farm.

- Horatio, after listening to a friend discuss his success in selling items through online auctions, began doing so himself. Starting as a hobby selling camping gear and novelty items through online auctions and on his own Web site, he grew his business to the point that he could quit is job.

- Rylie listened to her friends' encouragement and opened her antique and home accessories booth in an antique mall.

- After repeated requests from family and friends, Wyn increased production of her all-natural, homemade soaps and began marketing them through grocery stores and boutiques.

2.3   activity
suggestions from others

Other contacts

In addition to the family and friends you identified in Activity 2.2, what other contacts may be a rich source of ideas? Include neighbors, teachers, co-workers, club members, colleagues, and others.

a. List key members of your expanded network.

Name	Source of Relationship
1. _____	_____
2. _____	_____
3. _____	_____
4. _____	_____
5. _____	_____

b. Would any of the individuals listed above be a mentor or provide support to you in your entrepreneurial endeavors? If so, explain how.

c. Interview two to three individuals from the list above or from the list you identified in Activity 2.2 (the more the better) and ask them the questions on the next page.

Synthesis of suggestions from others

After completing the surveys on the next page, select the ideas that appeal to you the most. Tell why you selected these specific ones.

1. Name of Contact _____Relationship _____

a. What needs have you observed in the marketplace?

b. What types of products or services would you like to see offered in more variety? Of higher quality?

c. What problems have you experienced in meeting your personal consumer needs in the marketplace? Business needs?

d. If **you** were to start a business today, what type of business would you start and why?

2. Name of Contact _____Relationship _____

a. What needs have you observed in the marketplace?

b. What types of products or services would you like to see offered in more variety? Of higher quality?

c. What problems have you experienced in meeting your personal consumer needs in the marketplace? Business needs?

d. If **you** were to start a business today, what type of business would you start and why?

You may wish to make copies of this page to survey more people.

Other Sources

There are numerous possibilities for identifying business ideas, limited only by one's imagination, creativity, and awareness of your surroundings. The acronym **CHEC** will be used to refer to additional strategies that can be used.

Create   **H**unt for trends   **E**mulate others   **C**ritique

Create – Creativity is typically characterized by originality and imagination. In practice, however, the creative process is a way of reorganizing and reconfiguring objects and information in new and innovative ways. As Robert Sutton from Stanford University observed, every creative act he could identify consisted of doing new things with old things.

Hunt for trends – Trend identification is a systematic search for business ideas based on recent or enduring changes. It involves searching hard data to identify long-term shifts or movements in our society, economy, or marketplace. Many publications, including *Trends, Inc. Magazine,* and *Entrepreneur Magazine* publish trends for the coming year. Topping *Entrepreneur Magazine's* list of the hottest industries for 2008 were food and beverage and environmentally friendly products. By identifying trends early, you can spot growing needs and opportunities in the marketplace.

"If you are not early, you are late."
John R. Ortego

Emulate – Scan the marketplace to identify successful businesses that you might emulate or replicate. According to research reported by Amar Bhidē in his book *The Origin and Evolution of New Business*, most entrepreneurs start businesses by copying or slightly modifying someone else's idea. He goes on to state that it is not the idea itself but the excellent execution of the idea that differentiates business successes from failures.

Critique – Critiquing others businesses and remedying problems is another avenue to business success. Critiquing accompanies emulating, as entrepreneurs carefully scrutinize businesses in the marketplace.

CREATE

Creativity can be looked at on both an individual and process level. A creative individual frequently sees things differently from the way others see them. Sometimes we say creative people "think outside the box."

Entrepreneurs possess their own unique creativity in the way they perceive the world. Where many people see problems, entrepreneurs see potential opportunities. This was the case with Abby, whose observation of her employer's difficulty in communicating with his bilingual workforce coupled with her business and bilingual background, led her to start a business specializing in language translation and training for companies that hire large numbers of Hispanic workers.

The creative **person** is able to synthesize unrelated data to come up with original solutions. This creative **process** involves the following:
- Acquiring the appropriate knowledge or information.
- Synthesizing new information with existing knowledge into new patterns, a process often carried on at a subconscious level.
- Becoming aware of new patterns and knowledge.
- Verifying that a new idea will work through analysis and evaluation.

The story of George Mesral, the inventor of Velcor, is an excellent example of this creative process. On a walk through the woods, he noticed how cockleburs caught in his clothes and in his dog's fur. An engineer by trade, he decided to examine why they stuck so tightly. His observation and investigation led to the development of Velcro.

All people are creative to some extent. As a person grows older, the innate creativity of one's childhood diminishes. To test this premise, invite a 5-year-old child to accompany you outdoors to look at the clouds. A child's perception of all kinds of interesting animals and objects in the clouds is eye-opening, leaving the adult scratching his head in wonder at the child's imagination. Unfortunately, as a person ages, a number of social, emotional, and environmental factors negatively impact one's ability to tap the innate creativity with which they were born.

Diminishing creativity impacts the workplace as well as companies struggle to encourage innovation. Often creative breakthroughs come from people either new to an industry or from outside of a field. These individuals bring fresh and different viewpoints to problems and situations.

self check

What is it that blocks your creativity? Ask yourself, do I:

- Look for the one "right" answer?
- Fear rejection by others?
- Fear criticism by others?
- Fear failure?
- Rush to find an answer?

Some talented individuals are creative in an artistic sense—visual and performing artists, writers. Unless you're one of them, it's more likely your creativity exhibits itself in the way you live your everyday life, solving simple problems in new and innovative ways. One group of potential entrepreneurs, when pushed for examples of their own creativity, came up with several practical examples. An individual who stated he was about as creative as a "brick wall," talked about his ability to walk into an older home and envision how removing walls and adding windows would update and open the

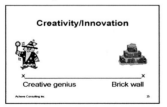

61

space to appeal to the contemporary home buyer.   Another young woman gave examples of her talent for developing new recipes.   Neither considered these abilities to be examples of creativity, which they were.

"First comes thought; then organization of that thought into ideas and plans, then transformation of those plans into reality. The beginning, as you will observe, is your imagination."

Napoleon Hill

Some entrepreneurs focus on coming up with new inventions, but more than likely they use their creativity to produce or market existing products or services in new and different ways. History shows that innovation rather than invention is more apt to reap financial rewards, especially in the short run. It's typically not the pioneers in a field who are the most successful financially, but rather those who follow.

For an extensive listing of resource materials on innovation and creativity, including numerous short videos by leading authorities and professors in the field, go to www.edcorner.stanford.edu and click on "Creativity and Innovation" listed under "Topics."

Forced Relationships
A simple process to stimulate your creative thinking, which you will use in Activity 2.4, is based on the concept of forcing relationships—putting things together that do not normally go together. Several retailers have been successful doing this is the past decade, such as Borders and Barnes & Noble Bookstores, including a coffee shop in their bookstores, and Target discount store offering Taco Bell and Starbucks at some of their locations.

Consider how this process can be used to identify new and creative ways to develop and market the products you are considering. What practices can you adopt from others businesses or industries that will result in a fresh, new, creative approach to offering your products or services in the marketplace.

- **Advertising and Promotion.** Studying the methods used by competitors will give you helpful hints as to what types of promotions have been effectively used in your industry. Studying different industries' advertising and promotional practices may provide the spark to help you think creatively about how to promote your products in a non-traditional manner. For example, how are health care plans marketed? Fitness clubs? Restaurants? New cars? Consulting services? Mary Kay Cosmetics? Can any of the methods of advertising and promoting a product in other industries apply to the product or service you plan to sell?

  In addition to the typical advertising methods of print, radio, and television, there is a vast array of other marketing options, such as event sponsorship, speaking engagements by the entrepreneur, personal sales calls, telemarketing, infomercials, and frequent-buyer programs, to name a few. Can you adopt any of these marketing techniques to your product or service?

- **Target Marketing.** Target markets are those customer groups that you identify to buy your products or services. Diagram 2.1 identifies common ways to segment consumer and business-to-business markets. The more clearly and precisely you define your target market, the more effective you will be in reaching it.

  A change in the selection of target markets may create a whole new opportunity, as was the case when office supply stores began targeting consumer markets instead of business markets. Retail giants such as Office Depot and Office Max capitalized on the boom in home offices as a result of the increasing number of employees working from their homes, self-employed individuals, and small businesses. Today prescription medicines, formerly marketed only to medical professionals, are now aggressively marketed via television and magazines to the public at large.

Market Segmentation

Consumer Markets (Business to Consumer [B to C])	Business Markets (Business to Business [B to B])

Consumer Markets
(Business to Consumer [B to C])

Business Markets
(Business to Business [B to B])

Geographic factors
    Where buyers are located
Demographic factors
    Age, gender, income, ethnicity, education, etc.
Psychological factors
    Buying motives, personality traits
Buying patterns
    Frequency, where purchases made
Lifestyle
    Single, early married, married with children,
    empty nesters, seniors, etc.

Location
Size
Industry

Diagram 2.1

- **Packaging.** One form of packaging is the physical box or container for products. Changes in this type of product packaging in the food industry introduced consumers to tuna in plastic pouches, juice in boxes, and cheese in zip-locked bags. When such innovative packaging hit the marketplace, the general reaction was, "Finally!" In another example of creative packaging, a famous author distributed his latest book one chapter at a time over the Internet. This was quite a change from selling his novels through major book retailers.

Packaging also refers to combining multiple products in one offering or bundling together services. For example, a custom home builder offered several buyer packages—varying levels of support to his clients. He worked with many home buyers from the initial planning stage through completion, providing the home to the buyer in finished form, ready to be inhabited. For others, he performed only the basic planning and construction, allowing home buyers to finish the projects on their own. In another example, a health club offered individual, family, and friendship memberships—allowing a second member to join for half the price of a normal membership.

Consider how the products or services you plan to sell may be packaged differently, learning from successful businesses in other industries.

- **Distribution.** Product and service distribution frequently changes with technology, as is the case of Internet marketing that has enabled consumers to buy everything from furniture and cars to financial products online. Dell™ Computers has been extremely successful marketing their computers over the Internet. Who would have thought a decade or so ago that consumers would be comfortable buying computers online? Other Internet retailing giants include eBay, Amazon.com, Barnes & Noble, and Borders Bookstore. Consider how you can distribute your products more effectively and efficiently.

C_{lips}

- Nicole changed the target market for her physical therapy practice from two-legged patients to four-legged ones, treating pets instead of people. Additional coursework in canine rehabilitation enabled her to make this transition.

- Leslie targeted corporate clients to expand her catering company beyond her current wedding and private-party markets.

- Mika used direct mail and a Web site to promote and sell her specialty ethnic bakery items.

HUNT FOR TRENDS

Do you know the difference between a trend and a fad? A trend refers to a general direction or tendency over a period of some duration. Synonyms of the word "fad" are "craze" and "whim."

For most businesses, long-term trends provide a solid foundation for long-term growth. By identifying major trends, a business can capitalize on the growth opportunities that will

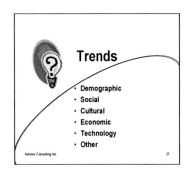

exist in the marketplace, possibly for years to come. This is the philosophy of catching the wave early and riding it until it crests. In this section, you will identify trends that provide an opportunity for sustained business development.

An entrepreneur whose business is based on a fad may, indeed, have a short-term business. For example, in Andrew's specialty store, his best-selling product line was a popular, collectible, children's stuffed toy. When customers' interests waned, sales significantly declined resulting in considerable financial hardship.

Some entrepreneurs intentionally focus on fads, developing short-term businesses to capitalize on them. Those starting ventures around the Olympic games know in advance that their business is short-run. Knowledge and planning are the keys.

Trends arise as a result of changes in a number of areas, such as demographics, technology, society, or economics. Demographics relates to the composition of the population, including factors such as age, ethnicity, and gender. Demographic trends help predict consumer and business spending patterns decades in advance. The baby boom that began in the late 1940s had a significant impact on the demand for education, housing, household appliances, cars, clothing, healthcare, and entertainment over the subsequent decades. Many successful businesses resulted from entrepreneurs anticipating the needs and wants of this massive group of consumers. As baby boomers age, the impact will be felt in the areas of changing housing needs, health care, and entertainment, to name a few.

The growth in the Hispanic and Asian populations in the United States is opening new markets for products and services targeting these groups. The increasing number of individuals living alone as a result of divorce or marrying later has had an impact on the housing industry.

Trends related to consumer products typically make themselves known in certain areas of the country before others. Clothing trends often appear in major cities on the East or West Coasts prior to reaching the heartland. New products and services often are offered in larger cities prior to becoming available in smaller ones.

One way to spot trends is to visit another city or look at their Yellow Pages and compare what is available there with what is available in the same product or service category in your area. Yellow Page information for other cities can be obtained over the Internet by accessing www.yellowpages.com. For example, if you are interested in starting a restaurant, look under restaurants in the Yellow Pages and compare the number and types of restaurants in your area to those in New York, Los Angeles, or other major metropolitan areas. A second approach is to identify a sister city – a city similar to yours in size, economics, and demographics, and complete the same activity described above, comparing what's available in your area to types and numbers of businesses in your sister city. Both of these techniques can help you identify products or services not available locally.

For most products or services, there is a window of opportunity in which those who enter the marketplace can take advantage of the growing demand. This typically coincides with the early stages of a trend. Knowledge of trends will help you anticipate and evaluate that window. For example, Dell™ has been extremely successful addressing the trend of mass customization and technology, building each computer to customer specifications while serving a global market. Catching a trend early is the key to sustained growth.

"Don't skate to the puck;
skate to where the puck is going to be."
Wayne Gretzsky, hockey player

Information on trends abounds. At the time of this writing, a search for books using the keyword "trends" on Amazon.com resulted in a listing of almost 300,000 books. In an Internet search for demographic trends, the keyword "demographics" yielded more than 400 titles. A visit to your local library will also result in finding many publications on trends. Some resources address the market and society as a whole; others are specific to industries or certain segments of the market.

Magazines and newspapers are also helpful sources of information. *Entrepreneur Magazine* and *Business Start-Up* magazine, among others, identify trends in entrepreneurship. Publications for specific industries or interest groups provide trend information, such as *Motor Trend* for the domestic and foreign car markets. Following is a sample of the types of resources available.

Trend Publications and Web Sites – A <u>sample</u> of resources:

Dictionary of the Future—The Words, Terms and Trends That Define the Way We Live, Work and Talk by Faith Popcorn and Adam Hanft, December 2001.

Demographics of the US, Trends and Projections by Cheryl Russell, November 2000.

Global Trends 2005, An Owners Manual for the Next Decade by Michael J. Mazarr, 2005.

Microtrends: The Small Forces Behind Tomorrow's Big Changes by Mark Penn and E. Kinney Zalesne, September 2007.

The 100 Best Trends, 2006: Emerging Developments You Can't Afford to Ignore, by George Ochoa and Melinda Corey, 2005.

The Extreme Future: The Top Trends That Will Reshape the World for the Next 5, 10, and 20 Years by James Canton, September 2006.

Think Forward, Get Ahead, and Cash in on the Future by Richard Laermer, 2002.

Trends (Tom Peters Essentials) by Tom Peters and Martha Barletta, May 2005.

<u>www.FreeDemographics.com</u>. 2000 Census Data, All Geographies and Radius Reports.

<u>www.trendwatching.com</u>. Consumer trends.

In Activity 2.5, you begin your search for business ideas by looking at demographic trends. In Activity 2.6 you identify societal, cultural, economic, and technical trends. It is highly recommended that you continue your search on your own after completing these activities.

"Prediction is difficult, especially about the future."

Yogi Berra

The examination of trends can be a lengthy process, as you will see by reading the following Snapshot.

Snapshot of Entrepreneur

Joe Edwards spent six months studying demographics and researching the demand for self-storage prior to building Four Seasons Self Storage, a climate- and non-climate-controlled storage for all kinds of storage needs.

Research relating to the mobility of the U.S. population and the number of possessions people accumulate convinced Joe there was a strong need for this type of business. Additionally, he discovered that there was excellent "exit potential" to sell the business to owners of similar properties. He received inquiries from others interested in purchasing the business before the buildings were even completed.

Clips

- Jill's difficult experience with finding affordable retirement living accommodations for elderly family members, combined with research regarding the aging population, convinced her of the opportunity presented in the marketplace for such facilities.

- Noting the difficulties that two-income families had transporting their children to and from after-school activities, orthodontic appointments, dance lessons and the like, Annette started an after-school transportation service to meet the needs of this target market.

- Rickeena, through her job as a manager of a large medical office, became aware of the many elderly individuals who had no close family members to assist them with financial and insurance matters. With the anticipated growth of this population, she started a business to handle these concerns for the elderly.

- Luis started a bookkeeping service for small businesses to capitalize on the growing number of home-based businesses.

EMULATE AND CRITIQUE

Although many entrepreneurs are looking for the big breakthrough idea, it is typically the simple, even mundane one that represents the greatest business opportunity. Rather than coming up with a totally new business idea, sometimes just repackaging, redesigning, or offering an existing product or service efficiently or in an innovative manner will lead to success. Especially when the product or service is experiencing significant sales growth, slight improvements or changes may attract new customers or increase sales to existing customers. By analyzing successful businesses and identifying their strengths and weaknesses, entrepreneurs can capitalize on winning ideas in the market.

It is not uncommon for the nascent or inexperienced entrepreneur to discount others' businesses and the loyalty of their customers. Remember, long-term business ventures are meeting consumers' needs at some level or they would not still be in business. Emulating what works and improving upon what doesn't can be a very effective way to launch a business.

Businesses that are only marginally successful also provide a rich learning opportunity. The astute investigator can identify weaknesses to be avoided and anticipate problems by studying these businesses.

> *"Many of life's failures are people who did not realize how close they were to success when they gave up."*
>
> Thomas A. Edison

By scanning the marketplace, entrepreneurs can identify products or services to replicate or ones that could succeed with a little fine tuning, modification, or better implementation. In Activity 2.8 you try your hand at applying this technique of improving upon others' ideas.

Clips

- Jun decided to start a business as a personal trainer, benefiting from several years of working in a health club. He was able to learn from his previous employers' mistakes, improving customer service and retention.

- Noting the success a popular coffee shop franchise, Hally, who had been a frequent customer, started her own coffee shop, providing gourmet coffee, delicious bakery items, and Internet access to local patrons.

- Working as an in-home health care worker motivated Antonio to start his own home health care service, focusing on better meeting the emotional and physical needs of his ageing clients.

2.4

activity
creativity

In this activity, you explore ways to be creative and innovative in your approach to marketing your favorite idea(s). You will use a process based on the concept of forced choice—putting together things that do not often or naturally occur together.

Choose one Business Idea (identify) _____

A. Advertising and promotion

Step 1. List the ways this product or service is commonly advertised or promoted in the marketplace.

Step 2. Brainstorm ways unrelated products or services are marketed (ones from other industries).

Step 3. Which of the methods identified in Step 2 would be an innovative approach to marketing the product or service you identified?

71

B. Target marketing

Step1: List the market(s) you would most likely target for the idea identified.

Step 2: What different target markets, if any, do competitors attract?

Step 3: Brainstorm markets that are <u>not</u> being targeted.

Step 4: Which target markets identified in Step 3 provide a new opportunity to market the products or services you identified?

C. Packaging

Step 1: List how competitors package their product or service.

Step 2: Brainstorm how products or services are packaged in other industries.

Step 3: Which of the methods you identified in Step 2 would be an innovative approach to packaging the product or service you identified?

D. Distribution

Step 1: List ways your products or services are typically distributed.

Step 2: Brainstorm methods of distribution used in other industries.

Step 2: Which of the methods identified in Step 2 would be an innovative approach to packaging the product or service identified?

Copy this and the previous two pages to repeat this process for other ideas.

Synthesis of creative marketing

Which of the variations identified above appear to have the most potential and why?

2.5

activity
demographic trends

Demographic trends

Review the demographic composition of your local community and our nation and search for significant demographic changes. An easy way to access this information is to go to your favorite Internet search engine and type in "demographic trends." A wealth of information is at your disposal.

Identify demographic information that represents significant opportunities for entrepreneurs. Reference the source of this information and brainstorm related business opportunities.

Demographic Data or Trend	Source of Information	Opportunity Presented
	Internet, name and date of publication – book, magazine, newspaper, etc.	Brainstorm list of ideas
Example		
The number of Hispanics in the US has more than doubled since 1980.	*Demographic Trends in the 20th Century, 2004; Hobbs and Stoops; US Census Bureau*	*Hispanic-oriented restaurants, grocery stores, magazines, newspapers, furniture, art, and home accessories*

Yours

1._____   _____   _____

_____

_____

_____

2._____ _____ _____

_____

_____

_____

3._____ _____ _____

_____

_____

_____

Synthesis of trends

Of the many ideas for businesses noted above, which one(s) appeals to you the most and why?

2.6

activity
trends – societal, cultural, economic, technical

Trend identification

After scanning the Internet and various printed sources related to societal, cultural, economic, or technical trends in general or in your area of interest in particular, identify three significant trends and brainstorm business ideas related to them.

Trend	Source Internet, name and date of publication – book, magazine, newspaper, etc.	Opportunity Presented Brainstorm list of ideas

Example

Young people are waiting longer to marry   *Star newspaper, January, 2006*   *Apartments, inexpensive dining, single-serving packaged food, home-repair services*

Yours

1._____   _____   _____

_____

_____

_____

2._____ _____ _____

_____

_____

_____

3._____ _____ _____

_____

_____

_____

Synthesis of trends

Of the many ideas for businesses noted above, which appeal to you the most and why?

2.7 activity
spotting trends before they reach your area

Trends related to consumer products will make themselves known in certain locations before others. Compare the listings in the product/service category you are considering in your local Yellow Pages with that of a different metropolitan area. Yellow Page information for other cities can be obtained over the Internet by accessing www.yellowpages.com. Note: It may be more difficult to conduct this activity if you are considering a business product. Locating information for business-to-business sales may require accessing trade or industry publications.

a. What is your area of interest?

b. What metropolitan area are you using as a comparison?

c. What new or different products/services did you find by comparing the Yellow Page listings in your local area with that of the metropolitan area you selected?

Synthesis of spotting trends

For any products or services identified in item "c" above, which one(s) presents a possible business opportunity in your trade area and why?

2.8 activity
making modifications

This activity gives you the opportunity to look around the marketplace and learn from both successful and not-so-successful businesses. Both can teach valuable lessons.

A. **Business Critique—How can this <u>successful</u> business be replicated, changed, or improved?**

Identify and visit the location, if possible, of a business in your area of interest that does things extraordinarily well or offers something unique. If the business you are interested in evaluating is not physically accessible (it is to far away to visit), analyze it by gathering information through literature and the Internet, or by talking to customers and vendors.

Name of Business _____

Location _____ Date of Visit _____

a. Description of product(s) or service(s):

b. What is the business doing right?

c. How would you modify, improve on, slightly change, or uniquely market the products or services of the business described above?

d. How could other aspects of the business be improved? (There is always room for improvement.)

B. Business Critique—How can this <u>not</u>-<u>so</u>-<u>successful</u> business be changed or improved?

Identify and visit the location, if possible, of a business in your area of interest that is struggling. If the business is not physically accessible (it is too far away to visit), analyze it by gathering information through literature and the Internet or by talking to customers and vendors.

Name of Business _____

Location _____ Date of Visit _____

a. Description of product(s) or service(s):

b. What is the business doing right? (Remember, if the business is still open, it is doing some things right.)

c. What is this business doing poorly?

d. How would you modify, improve on, slightly change, or uniquely market the products or services of the business described above?

e. How could other aspects of the business be improved or changed?

C. Synthesis of making modifications

What have you learned by analyzing these two businesses?

2.9 Step 2
synthesis of ideas generated by looking externally, activities 2.1- 2.8

Looking back over each of the activities in Step 2, list all ideas included in the Synthesis sections of 2.1 – 2.8.

2.10 Steps 1 and 2
Synthesis of ideas from looking both externally and internally

Review Step 1 Synthesis, Activity 1.5, and Step 2 Synthesis, Activity 2.9, and record below those ideas:
- About which you are most enthusiastic.
- That you feel have the greatest potential.
- That are most closely related to your work experience, education, skills, and talents.

Step 3

Screening Business Ideas

Step 3 Objective

To screen ideas on the basis of how they:

- Fit your talents and skills.

- Meet your personal and professional goals.

- Meet your financial goals.

- Address marketplace needs.

Matching Ideas with Skills and Talents

In this section, you will evaluate which of your many ideas are the best match for your personal strengths, interests, and talents. Some skills, such as sales or financial expertise, apply to a broad range of business opportunities. This allows the potential entrepreneur much latitude in the types of businesses to consider. Other skills, such as technical ones, may be narrower in scope and require the entrepreneur to look closely at related areas.

"Do what you excel in."
Author Unknown

In literature, descriptions of successful entrepreneurs usually include a combination of skills and characteristics. In this book, the word "skills" refers to expertise that can be learned through coursework, work experience, or mentoring by others. "Characteristics" and "talents" refer to qualities for which individuals possess an innate aptitude or predisposition. Entrepreneurial behaviors, such as opportunity recognition and networking, include both learned and innate components.

No one set of skills and characteristics is common to <u>all</u> entrepreneurs. However, certain ones are crucial to entrepreneurial success. These include:

- Sensitivity to and awareness of opportunities in the marketplace

- Persuasiveness and ability to network with others
- Determination and passion
- Fundamental knowledge of the financial aspects of the business
- Awareness of the importance of marketing and the ability to market a good or service or the willingness to find others to do so.

The title of an article by serial entrepreneur Jack Roseman, "Entrepreneurs Who Make It; Key Traits Are Perseverance, Communication Skills, People Knowledge, Ability to Distinguish Opportunities from Ideas," highlights the skills and talents this successful entrepreneur feels are critical to success. Although not all inclusive, the title of Roseman's article certainly identifies key skills and talents that you will want to assess in yourself.

> "use what talents you possess:
> the woods would be very silent if no birds sang there
> except those that sang best."
>
> Henry Van Dyke, poet

All individuals have strengths. A business idea that fits you should capitalize on yours. For those areas in which you do not excel, you will need to either acquire the necessary skills and knowledge or identify others who have them.

A word of caution –– although you can learn to perform skills for which you have little or no natural inclinations or abilities, it often takes a huge investment of time and energy to do so, sometimes with questionable results. The author of this book, for example, could edit and proofread her own material; but because of her innate dislike for and inattention to detail, it makes more sense for her to hire this expertise than do it herself. The same goes for keeping the books for her business. Although she has taken accounting courses and even taught it, she has no desire to keep her own books; yet like any other entrepreneur, she must have the ability to read financial statements and interpret the data her accountant provides to guide her business.

Are you right-handed or left-handed? Depending on your answer, now pick up a pen or pencil with your **other hand** and write your name.

- How does your name look?
- With repeated practice, could you eventually learn to write well with your other hand?
- Would writing with your other hand take more time and energy than writing with the hand you naturally use?

This simple Self Check can help simulate the difficulty of learning skills for which you have little or no ability. Although not impossible, it can be challenging.

The nice thing about entrepreneurship is that it is a team sport. Entrepreneurs utilize others to balance out their skills and expertise. An objective self assessment is the first step. The entrepreneur may then decide to take classes to develop skills that are lacking, have others mentor him or her, hire someone who possesses needed skills, contract with outside experts, or look for these skills in partners and management team members. By doing this, the entrepreneur can ensure that critical attributes are present within the organization.

Snapshot of Entrepreneur

Let's revisit Susan Davidson and see how uniquely qualified she is to start a business coaching foreign managers and executives working in the United States. You read about Susan's business, Beyond Borders, earlier. Evaluating herself on the skills inventory and the characteristics checklist in this section, Susan assessed her strongest skills as follows (X indicates strength):

Inventory – skills

a. Checkmark those items below that represent your strengths.

_____ analytical	_X_ communication
_X_ customer oriented	____ computer skills
_X_ creative/artistic	____ financial knowledge
____ implementation skills	_X_ event planning
____ listening	_X_ leadership
____ market awareness	____ marketing

___ meeting facilitation	_X_ networking
_X_ organizational	_X_ relationship building
___ research	_X_ public speaking
_X_ sales	___ tactical planning (near-term)
___ strategic planning (long-term)	___ team building
___ time management	_X_ other (list)
___ technical (specify)	_Cross cultural knowledge_
Languages	_____
_____	_____

Inventory – Personal Characteristics

b. Checkmark those items below that describe you.

_X_ achievement orientation	___ calculated risk taker
_X_ confidence in self	_X_ passion
_X_ perseverance	_X_ seeks feedback from others
_X_ comfortable with ambiguity	_X_ self starter

Reviewing Susan's strengths, you can see that her venture, Beyond Borders, is a good match for her skills and talents.

"Natural ability without education
has more often attained to glory and virtue than education
without natural ability."

Cicero, Roman author, orator, and politician

C_{lips}

- Angela's financial and marketing expertise led her to seek out businesses that were in trouble and which she could acquire, turn around, and sell.

- Nick gradually acquired multiple small apartment buildings, which he managed himself. His strong sense of independence, financial acumen for buying properties when the price was right, and skills in repair work contributed to his business success.

- Mitch, a young entrepreneur, started a small self-storage center in his hometown after graduating from high school. Utilizing his considerable marketing talents, high energy, and ability to identify a market need, he later enlarged this facility to accommodate more customers.

3.1 activity
matching ideas with skills and characteristics

Now is the time to reflect on all the hard work you have done. You have generated many ideas for a business based on your personal strengths, interests, talents and work experiences. You have looked to family and friends for possible mutually beneficial business associations. You have thoroughly observed and examined your environment for trends, creative ways of doing things, and ways to improve upon what is currently being done. Now it is time to complete an in-depth analysis of how key ideas capitalize on your skills and talents.

Directions: Inventory

Step 1: Personal Assessment. Assess your own skills and characteristics by completing the inventory on the next page. Review activities 1.1, 1.2, and 1.3, which highlight your talents and skills, prior to doing so.

Step 2: Peer Assessment. Make copies of the Peer Assessment form and ask two or more friends or family members to assess YOUR skills and characteristics by completing the inventory.

Step 3: Composite Inventory. Combine your Self Assessment with the Peer Assessments on the form identified as Composite Inventory.

Step 4: After you have completed your Composite Inventory, identify your areas of strength.

Step 5: After you have identified your strengths, identify which ideas in Activity 2.10, Synthesis of Steps 1 and 2, best utilize your strengths. List at least three ideas.

3.1 Step 1– Personal Assessment matching ideas with skills and characteristics

Directions: Assess your own skills and characteristics. Review activities 1.1, 1.2, and 1.3, which highlight your talents and skills, prior to completing.

Skills

a. Checkmark those items below that represent your strengths.

___ analytical	___ communication
___ customer oriented	___ computer skills
___ creative/artistic	___ financial knowledge
___ implementation skills	___ event planning
___ listening	___ leadership
___ market awareness	___ marketing
___ meeting facilitation	___ networking
___ organizational	___ relationship building
___ research	___ public speaking
___ sales	___ tactical planning (short-term)
___ strategic planning (long-term)	___ team building
___ time management	___ other (list)
___ technical (specify)	

_____   _____

_____   _____

_____   _____

_____   _____

Personal Characteristics

b. Checkmark those items below that describe you.

___ achievement orientation	___ calculated risk taker
___ confidence in self	___ passion
___ perseverance	___ seeks feedback from others
___ comfortable with ambiguity	___ self starter

3.1 Step 2 – Peer Assessment matching ideas with skills and characteristics

Directions: Ask two or more friends/relatives to complete this assessment.

Skills

a. Checkmark those items below that represent your strengths.

____ analytical	____ communication
____ customer oriented	____ computer skills
____ creative/artistic	____ financial knowledge
____ implementation skills	____ event planning
____ listening	____ leadership
____ market awareness	____ marketing
____ meeting facilitation	____ networking
____ organizational	____ relationship building
____ research	____ public speaking
____ sales	____ tactical planning (short-term)
____ strategic planning (long-term)	____ team building
____ time management	____ other (list)
____ technical (specify)	

_____ _____

_____ _____

_____ _____

_____

Personal Characteristics

b. Checkmark those items below that describe you.

____ achievement orientation	____ calculated risk taker
____ confidence in self	____ passion
____ perseverance	____ seeks feedback from others
____ comfortable with ambiguity	____ self starter

3.1 Step 2 – Peer Assessment matching ideas with skills and characteristics

Directions: Ask two or more friends/relatives to complete this assessment.

Skills

a. Checkmark those items below that represent your strengths.

____ analytical
____ customer oriented
____ creative/artistic
____ implementation skills
____ listening
____ market awareness
____ meeting facilitation
____ organizational
____ research
____ sales
____ strategic planning (long-term)
____ time management
____ technical (specify)

____ communication
____ computer skills
____ financial knowledge
____ event planning
____ leadership
____ marketing
____ networking
____ relationship building
____ public speaking
____ tactical planning (short-term)
____ team building
____ other (list)

_____
_____
_____

_____
_____
_____

Personal Characteristics

b. Checkmark those items below that describe you.

____ achievement orientation
____ confidence in self
____ perseverance
____ comfortable with ambiguity

____ calculated risk taker
____ passion
____ seeks feedback from others
____ self starter

Make copies of page for additional assessments.

3.1 Step 3 – Composite matching ideas with skills and characteristics

Directions: Combine your personal assessment with that of your peer assessments.

Skills

a. Checkmark those items below that represent your strengths.

___ analytical	___ communication
___ customer oriented	___ computer skills
___ creative/artistic	___ financial knowledge
___ implementation skills	___ event planning
___ listening	___ leadership
___ market awareness	___ marketing
___ meeting facilitation	___ networking
___ organizational	___ relationship building
___ research	___ public speaking
___ sales	___ tactical planning (near-term)
___ strategic planning (long-term)	___ team building
___ time management	___ other (list)
___ technical (specify)	

_____   _____
_____   _____
_____   _____
_____   _____

Personal Characteristics

b. Checkmark those items below that describe you.

___ achievement orientation	___ calculated risk taker
___ confidence in self	___ passion
___ perseverance	___ seeks feedback from others
___ comfortable with ambiguity	___ self starter

3.1   Step 4 Strengths matching ideas with skills and characteristics

Strengths: After you have completed your Composite Inventory in Step 3, identify your strengths below.

3.1 Step 5 Matching ideas with skills and characteristics

Matching: Based on your Composite Inventory, Step 3, and strengths identified in Step 4, which ideas listed in Activity 2.10 best utilize your abilities? Identify at least three ideas below.

Evaluating Ideas:
Personal, Professional, and Financial Goals, Market Viability

What makes an idea for a business a good one? A good idea is right for you and for the marketplace. It is an idea for which the financial and emotional rewards far outweigh the risks. It is an idea that you have the talents and expertise to accomplish—you evaluated this aspect of viability in the previous section. A good idea fulfills your personal and professional dreams and goals. It is one for which you have the funds or can pull together the finances to launch. And it is an idea that fulfills a market need. In this section, you will begin to evaluate your business idea(s) in all of these areas.

Of the many ideas you identified, now is the time to pare them down to a manageable few that warrant further exploration.

"A mediocre idea that generates enthusiasm will go further than a great idea that inspires no one."

Mary Kay Ash

PERSONAL AND PROFESSIONAL GOALS

By visualizing what you wish to accomplish and having clear goals to lead you in that direction, you can greatly increase the likelihood of succeeding. Many books have been written on this and the power of positive thinking. What are the goals and dreams you have for your future?

A number of years ago at the summer Olympics in Sydney, Australia, Maurice Greene, the world-famous track star, was overheard repeatedly saying to himself before a race, "I'm the fastest man in the world; I'm the fastest man in the world." Maurice Greene's father, upon hearing Maurice, said to the reporter interviewing him, "He's at it again. Maurice has been saying this since he was a little boy." Obviously, Maurice Greene had the ability to dream big and visualize his success from a very young age.

Will your business lead you to fulfill your goals and dreams—a business is not an end in itself but rather a means to achieving the life you wish to lead. There is life before, during, and after a business. In Activity 3.1, you reflect on what you want your life to look like during the time you run your business and afterwards. What does personal and professional fulfillment mean to you? What would it look like? What would you be doing? Enjoying? Accomplishing? What would your lifestyle be? Only you can evaluate whether your business idea will lead to the life you want.

FINANCIAL GOALS

Closely aligned to your personal and professional goals are your financial goals, which you clarify in Activity 3.2. Here, too, money is not an end in itself but a means to an end—the goals you have for your life. Rarely do entrepreneurs cite money as the reason they started their businesses. The desire to be their own boss and to pursue a passion are what entrepreneurs repeatedly say is their motivation. Money is the by-product of pursuing one's dreams.

Although money may not be the primary motivator, it is important that the financial rewards of having your own business are adequate for the life you desire. It is also critical that the entrepreneur have a solid understanding of the financial potential of a proposed business. Just as some careers provide more financial rewards than others, businesses also differ in the financial potential they provide. Knowing this proved beneficial to one middle aged woman taking a business plan course who was contemplating opening a candle shop in the local mall.

Detailed financial projections showed her that the most income she could hope to make in the proposed venture was approximately $50,000 a year. Based on this analysis, she decided to wait to start a business until she came up with a concept that would generate $80,000 a year. That was the amount she felt she needed to maintain her lifestyle and to compensate her for giving up her current job and undertaking the risks of starting her own business.

MARKET VIABILITY

At the center of an opportunity is an idea, but not all ideas are opportunities. Market viability is the litmus test for determining if a business idea is really a business opportunity. Does a market exist for the product or service you are considering? Will anyone want to buy it? Can you sell it at a price at which you can make a profit?

Look around you for evidence of market acceptance of your idea. Are others successfully offering your product or service? Are customers identifiable and ready to buy?

self check

Ask yourself: Does my product or service
- meet a need in the marketplace?
- solve a problem for the consumer?
- fulfill a want of the consumer?
- fill a market niche?

The concept of product life cycle is helpful in determining the overall market viability of a product. Product life cycle was popularized by Alvin Toffler in the 1960s, and subsequent research, as reported in the article, "Shortening of the PLC: An Empirical Test" by William Qualls, Richard W. Olshavsky, and Ronald E. Michaels, showed life cycles rapidly getting shorter as early as the 1980's. Advances in technology in more recent decades has only intensified this process.
- Introduction (or development) stage. Substantial costs have been incurred to develop and test the product. Products/services are first being introduced into the marketplace and typically require extensive amounts of capital for educating the market and promotion. It is unlikely that a business will make profits at this stage.
- Growth stage. Customers are knowledgeable about the product and are ready to buy. The marketplace is increasingly demanding more of the product and there is room for additional

new businesses as sales and profits rapidly increase. One important consideration at this stage is whether or not you will be able to set your business apart from others in the market.

- Maturity stage. Demand remains relatively stable or decreases. More and more providers are meeting the needs of customers. This often results in aggressive competition and price cutting. The increasing number of competitors, many large and well established, often necessitates that small businesses specialize or focus on smaller niche markets. Personal customer service, an advantage that small businesses can have over their larger counterparts, is the key to attracting and keeping customers.

- Decline stage. This stage is characterized by decreasing product demand and producers leaving the marketplace. At this point, one should seriously question entering the market. In some situations, however, research may reveal that there is still growth potential in a specific trade area, running counter to the declining demand in a regional or national market.

The concept of product life cycle may be helpful for planning purposes, tempered with caution related to the unpredictability of the marketplace. New businesses often have the greatest opportunity for success in the growth stage of the life cycle. The relatively high demand and profit margins allow for both business growth and the early miscalculations common in new businesses.

"often the difference between a successful man and a failure is not one's better abilities or ideas but the courage that one has to bet on his ideas, to take a calculated risk – and act."

Maxwell Maltz

Many ideas will not survive the close scrutiny that you apply in this section. For those ideas that do survive, you will conduct basic market research to obtain confirmation of market viability.

3.2 activity
screening – personal and professional goals and dreams

A. My personal goals and dreams

In looking ahead, visualize what you want your life to be like. What will you be doing? What will your lifestyle be? Take into account factors such as your age, your stage of life—early adulthood (20–29), middle years (30–49), nearing retirement (50–65), retirement (66+)—and the age of your loved ones.

a. Visualize life in 5 years.
   How old will you be? _____ What would you like your personal life to be like?

b. Visualize life in 10 years.
   How old will you be? _____ What would you like your personal life to be like?

c. Visualize life in 20 years.
   How old will you be? _____ What would you like your personal life to be like?

B. My professional goals and dreams

a. Visualize life in 5 years.
   How old will you be? _____   What would you like your professional life to be like?

b. Visualize life in 10 years.
   How old will you be? _____   What would you like your professional life to be like?

c. Visualize life in 20 years.
   How old will you be? _____   What would you like your professional life to be like?

C. My goals and dreams screening

Which of the ideas that you identified earlier in Activity 3.1 (Matching Ideas with Skills and Characteristics) are most compatible with the personal and professional goals and dreams identified above?

3.3 activity screening – financial goals

A. My current financial needs

I require the following income to support my current lifestyle. (Do not include what others in your household may generate.)

( ) $0 - $25,000 per year   ( ) $26 - $50,000 per year

( ) $51 - $75,000 per year   ( ) $76 - $100,000 per year

( ) more than $100,000 per year

B. My future financial needs

I need the following income to support my planned future lifestyle and goals.

( ) $0 - $25,000 per year   ( ) $26 - $50,000 per year

( ) $51 - $75,000 per year   ( ) $76 - $100,000 per year

( ) more than $100,000 per year

C. My personal net worth is

Assets are items of value and may be liquid or fixed. Examples of liquid assets include cash (money in a checking or savings account), and near cash (investments that can be converted into cash relatively easily, like stocks and bonds). Examples of fixed assets are your home and car. Liabilities are claims against assets—the mortgage on your house, what you owe the bank on your car, and so on. Answer the following questions regarding your assets and liabilities.

a. Estimate of my liquid assets (cash or near cash equivalents) $_____

b. Estimate of other assets (real estate, cars, etc.) $_____

c. Estimate of my total liabilities—what I owe $_____

d. My total net worth *$_____
   Subtract your total liabilities (c) from your total assets (a + b). The remainder is your net worth.

e. I am willing to invest ____ percent of my net worth in a business.
   Remember, not all of your net worth is liquid.

f. Total amount in dollars that I am willing to invest: *$_____
   Multiply your net worth, item "d," by the percentage in item "e."

D. Other financial resources

In addition to what you are personally willing to invest in your business, what other funding can you obtain? Personal savings and money from family and friends are the most common sources of funding for start-up businesses. An early analysis of your network of family members and friends as potential investors and/or sources of loan dollars is helpful as you plan the funding of your business.

Source of Funding	Approximate Amount
_____	$_____
_____	$_____
_____	$_____
_____	$_____
_____	$_____

g. Total amount of money I can obtain from others $_____

h. Total amount of money from all sources $_____
   Add together personal investment, item "f" on previous page, and funding from others, item "g".

Note: Funding from sources such as banks and venture capitalists is not generally available at the concept and start-up stages of business development.

E. Synthesis of personal financial screening

Evaluate those ideas listed in Activity 3.2, item "C" – My goals and dreams screening, to see which have the most potential to meet your financial needs now and in the future and which you have the resources to start. *Note: A detailed financial analysis will need to be undertaken to accurately assess the financial potential of your various ideas.*

List your top ideas here.

3.4

activity
screening – preliminary
market viability assessment

For each idea still remaining (Activity 3.3, item "E" – Synthesis of personal financial screening), complete a preliminary market viability assessment. Answer the questions below to the best of your ability based on your knowledge of the marketplace at this time.

Talking to people in the field and conducting basic market research will need to be completed to truly assess market viability, but considering these questions now will help you begin thinking about key market variables. *Note: Revisit this activity after completing activities 4.1 – 4.4 in Step 4. Some of your answers may change as a result of your market research..*

A. Market viability Idea #1_____

Circle Yes or No

Yes   No   1. Is the product or service unique or is there a perceived need for it?

Yes   No   2. Is there a clearly identified target market (those to whom you plan to sell)? If yes, describe: _____
_____

Yes   No   3. Does the target market have the ability to buy your product or service at a price that will provide an adequate profit?

Yes   No   4. Does the marketplace need another provider of this product or service?

Yes   No   5. Is the demand for this product or service relatively strong?

Yes   No   6. Are the growth projections for sales strong?

Yes   No   7. Will you have a sustainable competitive advantage (something in which you excel)? If yes, what is it? _____

Yes   No   8. Is there strong evidence of market acceptance of the product or service? If yes, what is it?_____

Yes   No   9. Do you have the ability to produce and sell enough of the product or service to be a profitable business?

Yes   No   10. Is there a way to easily reach the targeted market?

Total number of yes answers _____

B. Market viability Idea #2_____

Circle Yes or No

Yes No   1. Is the product or service unique or is there a perceived need for it?

Yes No   2. Is there a clearly identified target market (those to whom you plan to sell)? If yes, describe: _____

_____

Yes No   3. Does the target market have the ability to buy your product or service at a price that will provide an adequate profit?

Yes No   4. Does the marketplace need another provider of this product or service?

Yes No   5. Is the demand for this product or service relatively strong?

Yes No   6. Are the growth projections for sales strong?

Yes No   7. Will you have a sustainable competitive advantage (something in which you excel)? If yes, what is it? _____

Yes No   8. Is there strong evidence of market acceptance of the product or service? If yes, what is it?_____

Yes No   9. Do you have the ability to produce and sell enough of the product or service to be a profitable business?

Yes No 10. Is there a way to easily reach the targeted market?

Total number of yes answers _____

If assessing more than two ideas, make a photocopy of this page.

C. Synthesis of market viability

Which of your ideas had the highest score (number of yes answers circled)?

3.5

activity
Your No.1 Idea – The Key

Which business idea most successfully completed the screening process?

a. Identify your No.1 idea.

b. Describe your No. 1 idea briefly. What will your product or service look like?

c. How do you feel about the idea listed above? Is it a type of business you would like to start? Would you feel comfortable? Knowledgeable? Excited?

d. What other ideas (from previous lists) will you keep for possible further consideration?

3.6

activity
supporting trends for
No. 1 idea

For your No. 1 idea, scan various printed sources and the Internet to identify any trends that support your premise that your business idea has market viability. Trend identification can provide support that your idea is one for which the timing is right.

The Key – Your No. 1 Idea: _____

<u>Supporting Trends</u>	<u>Source</u>
	Name and date of source—book magazine, newspaper, Internet

1. _____   _____

2. _____   _____

3. _____   _____

4. _____   _____

Step 4

Further Investigation and Getting Started

Step 4 Objectives

To research your No. 1 business idea by:
- Surveying members of your target market.
- Conducting a competitive and environmental scan.
- Identifying a related trade or professional association.

To take the initial steps of getting started by:
- Identifying your first customer.
- Contacting a potential mentor.

Further Investigation

As you saw when you completed the previous market viability assessment, without hard data you are making an educated guess, at best, as to the market's response to your product or service.

Successful entrepreneurs engage in research before starting their businesses; typically, the more research, the better. Being calculated risk takers and practical by nature, entrepreneurs are looking for verification that they should proceed. Success at each step, and targeted research regarding the next one, propels entrepreneurs from one stage of business development and start-up to another.

The research you will conduct in this section is necessary to develop your business idea into a business concept. According to Dictionary.com, an idea is "your intention; what you intend to do." A concept is "a scheme; a plan." Converting an intention into a plan takes research.

A business concept identifies not only your product, but to whom you plan to sell, why they will buy from you, and how you will promote and distribute your product. The greater the risk involved, the more in-depth the research required. But even for a supposedly low-risk venture, such as bookkeeping or child care services, there are hidden costs in terms of lost time, energy, and income. With that in mind, all concepts warrant careful investigation.

115

"Basic research is what I am doing when I don't know what I am doing."

Wernher von Braun

TARGET MARKETS

To whom will you sell? Entrepreneurs need to very specifically identify the market they intend to target in order to develop their product to meet its needs and to be able to effectively reach it. Anytime an entrepreneur says that **everyone** is his or her intended market, there is cause for concern. This usually means, "I don't really know who the majority of my customers will be."

As shown in Diagram 2.1 earlier in the book, target markets may be either consumer (business to consumer) or business (business to business). Consumer markets are frequently segmented by geographic, demographic and psychographic variables. Business markets are typically segmented by geographic area, size, and industry. Can you describe your intended target market using these variables?

self check

Will I sell my product to a consumer market or business market? Depending on how you answer this question, respond to the appropriate set of questions below.

Consumer	Business
For potential customers:	For potential customers:
1. In what geographic area do they reside?	1. In what geographic area are most located?
2. What age range is representative of the **majority** of them?	2. In what industry(ies) are the majority?
3. What income level is representative of the **majority** of them?	3. What is the typical size of business?
4. What is their most typical lifestyle?	
5. What is their mindset?	

For example, the author of this book identified the primary target market for *Opportunity Analysis* as a business market and answered the questions above as follows:

1. The geographic area of the target market is national.
2. The industry is education, specifically the community college market.
3. The size of community colleges is medium to large.

Even though buyers of *Opportunity Analysis* also include small colleges and some state agencies, the **majority** of customers are medium to large community colleges.

Most small businesses use a focused marketing strategy initially, identifying one particular target market for their product. As they grow, they may begin using a differentiated marketing strategy, identifying more than one target market and adapting their product and promotional efforts to reach those markets.

MARKET RESEARCH – SURVEYS

Prior to your writing a full-blown business plan and launching a business, basic market research can enable you to test your business concept to determine whether or not to pursue a specific business idea. In your survey, you will attempt to identify what features are important to your buyer and what benefits are valued. The features of the watch on you arm might include 14 K solid gold link band, mother-of-pearl dial, Swiss quartz movements, numbered face, time and date, and so on. The benefits depend to some extent on the buyer, but would likely include convenience, dependability, and style. Customers buy benefits; many entrepreneurs, especially inexperienced ones, think in terms of features.

In this section, you will survey your target market—the customer group to which you plan to sell. Response rates to surveys vary drastically depending on whom you survey, their level of interest in your product, and their relationship to you. Therefore, you may need to survey many people to obtain the number of responses desired.

To help you in preparing your survey, you will first test it by administering it orally to a small number of people. After making the revisions to the survey that this test reveals, you will then prepare a written version to administer to a larger number of members of your target market.

At this point in time, some nascent entrepreneurs become particularly uncomfortable with the idea of telling others about their business idea. Their biggest fear is that someone will steal it.

This is sometimes referred to as "entrepreneurial paranoia" for lack of a better term. Although you may have a legitimate concern and need to take **reasonable** steps to protect yourself, the bigger risk is operating in a vacuum. For example, you would not want to share your idea with individuals who have skills very similar to yours and could easily copy your idea, but those individuals are probably rare. But you do want to obtain market feedback from potential buyers. At some time in the future your business will go public (open it doors), and everyone will know about your business and products.

COMPETITIVE AND ENVIRONMENTAL ANALYSIS

Conducting a competitive and environmental assessment is an important step in determining the overall timeliness of launching a particular type of business and evaluating the business climate.

Competitive Scan

Look at the marketplace and identify businesses that offer products that are the same or similar to what you plan to offer. It is important that you identify both your direct and indirect competition. For example, direct competitors for a greeting card shop are other greeting card shops. Indirect competition includes businesses that offer greeting cards as a sideline, such as grocery stores, gift shops, and even full-service car washes that have racks of greeting cards for customers to peruse while they wait. Both direct and indirect competitors compete for consumer dollars.

Direct competitors for a food caterer company, specializing in weddings and large corporate events, are other catering companies addressing these markets. Who are their indirect competitors? (Did you think about churches, relatives, friends, grocery stores that prepare and deliver food, restaurants, hotels, and so on? Any of these might make and serve food.)

When someone says they do not have competition, they usually mean they have no "direct" competition.

You can learn a great deal from your competitors. All too many entrepreneurs fall in the trap of discounting their competition. Remember, competitors would not still be in business if they were not doing some things right.

Environmental Analysis

The world in which small businesses operate is constantly changing. In the Introduction section of this book, the concept of creative destruction and the bubble theory (booms and busts) referenced the constant state of change that exemplifies the marketplace. A small firm's ability to respond to change quickly can be a source of considerable competitive strength as compared to their larger corporate counterparts. Anticipation and awareness of environmental changes allow small businesses to be proactive instead of reactive.

A great deal of information can be obtained through trade associations and industry journals and publications related to your business and industry. To identify a relevant trade association, surf the Internet or Google for trades associations. Or visit your local library and ask the reference librarian for the *Encyclopedia of Trade Associations*. An examination of your local Yellow Pages may enable you to identify a local chapter of a national association related to your business. Contact the association to acquire specific information about your industry's growth, trends, and conferences.

A lot of information about an industry is classified by Standard Industrial Classification (SIC) or North American Industry Classification System (NAICS) code. Both categorize businesses by types of products or services. NAICS is a more recent and comprehensive classification system that includes a larger number of service and technology businesses. For SIC code information, go to the U.S. Occupational Safety and Health Administration's (OSHA's) Web site at www.osha.gov/pls/imis/sicsearch.html. NAICS codes may be obtained by visiting the U.S. Census Bureau's Web site at http://www.census.gov/epcd/naics02/. Knowing your SIC and NAICS codes enables you to access information about your industry as well as other companies in the classification. The Resource listing at the end of this book provides sources of additional information about your industry and the macro- and micro-environment in which your business will operate.

Macro-Environmental Analysis. This is a "big picture" assessment of the business environment. Elements of the macro environment that are particularly relevant to small business include economic, regulatory, competitive, technological, demographic, social, and industry.

An industry's life cycle follows closely that of its products: introduction, growth, maturity, and decline. For example, the automobile is a "mature" product, and the automobile industry is a "mature" industry.

Micro-Environmental Analysis. This assessment focuses on the environment within the particular trade area in which your business will operate. Elements in the micro environment that are of particular importance to small business include regulations, economics, population trends, suppliers, and competition. Information may come from sources such as:

- Census data, county and city data
- *Survey of Buying Power* (*Sales and Marketing Management* magazine)
- Chambers of commerce
- Trade association reports and journals

Before investing your time and hard-earned cash in a business venture, isn't it worth it to conduct this type of basic market research?

activity
concept testing –
oral survey

Overview

Test your No. 1 idea by asking several potential customers, members of your target market, for feedback. This oral survey will aid you in the development of a more in-depth written survey. In developing your oral survey, follow these steps:

Oral Survey Preparation

- **Plan.** What do you want to find out? Develop a draft of the survey.
- **Administer.** Give oral survey to a small number of respondents and ask for feedback on content and questions.

Oral Survey Content

- **Description of product or service.** Start with a brief, written description of your product or service as you envision it.
- **Method of promotion.** Ask how customers would locate your type of business or product. Would they look in the phone book? Ask others? Look at ads? Ask why and how customers will purchase your product or service.
- **Features and benefits.** Ask potential customers what features are important to them? Why are these features important? What benefits do they provide?
- **Pricing.** Ask potential customers what they would be willing to pay. *Note: Questions regarding price can assist you in quantifying the perceived value of your product to buyers. It can also help you determine if you can sell your product or service at a profit. A survey response, however, may not predict actual consumer behavior. The true test is when potential customers open their billfold and make a purchase.*
- **Demographic data.** Collect information from respondents about <u>relevant</u> demographic variables—age, gender, residence, profession, and so on.

It is often just as helpful to find out why individuals will NOT buy your product as why they will. Probe negative responses.

activity
concept testing –
oral survey

In preparing for the survey, do the following:

Step 1. Complete the **top portions** of sections "A", "B", "C", "D" and "E".

Step 2. Interview at least three individuals by reading the top portion in each section and asking the corresponding survey question(s).

Step 3. Write respondents' answers in the box included in each section.

Step 4. At the completion of the survey, ask each respondent to provide feedback regarding the clarity and content of the survey's questions.

A. **Description.** Briefly describe your product or service idea.

_____

_____

_____

A. Share description with respondent.

Survey Question
1. Would you purchase this product or service? ___ Yes___ No

   If **yes**, continue with items "B" through "G".

   If **no**, ask, "Why not?"

B. **Marketing Methods.** List types of marketing planned (sales, advertising, and promotion).

a. _____

b. _____

c. _____

d. _____

B. Share marketing methods with respondent.

Survey Questions
1. Which marketing methods would be most effective in reaching you?
    (How would you expect to find out about my product or service? Where would you look for my product or service?)

2. What marketing methods might be effective in reaching others?

C. **Features.** List the specific parts or components of your product or service.

a. _____

b. _____

c. _____

d. _____

C. Share features with respondent and ask respondent to answer based on his or her preferences or perception of others' preferences.

Survey Questions
1. Which features are most valuable (to you or others) and why?

2. What other features would you like to see included?

D. **Benefits**. List anticipated benefits to the customer.

a. _____

b. _____

c. _____

D. Share anticipated customer benefits with respondent.

Survey Questions
1. Which benefits are of greatest value (to you or others) and why?

2. Are there other benefits that I have not identified?

E. Pricing

Indicate the price or price range (low, medium, or high relative to similar products or services in the market) you plan to charge.

E. Pricing

Select option "a" below if you have a specific price in mind. Select option "b" below if you have a price range in mind (low, medium, high). Ask all respondents the last question.

Option a
Survey Questions – Specific Price
1. At _____ (*tell price*) would you buy this product/service?

2. What is the most you would be willing to pay?

Option b
Survey Questions – Price Range
1. The price for my product/service will be _____ (low, high or average) compared to similar products/services. Would you buy at that price?

2. What is the most you would be willing to pay?

All respondents
Survey Question – Increasing Price
1. What factors would justify my charging a higher price (or positioning myself higher in the price range)?

F. Quantity

F. Survey Question
Approximately how many purchases of this product or service would you make in a year? *Note: Omit this question if purchase would likely be a one time event.*

G. Demographic information about respondent

Demographic questions might include: "What is your age (give ranges)? How many family members live in your household? What is your educational level (high school, some college, college degree, graduate school)? What is your income level (give ranges)? In what area of the city or country do you live? *Remember, respondents are more apt to answer questions of a personal nature, like age or income, if they are given a range to which to respond.*

Write questions about <u>relevant</u> demographic information below.

_____

_____

_____

G. Demographic information
Ask questions listed above and record respondents' answers

4.2

activity concept testing – written survey

A. Develop Written Survey

Based on feedback and information obtained through your oral survey, develop a written survey to administer to enough individuals to obtain a minimum of 10 completed surveys (20 would be better). If you were conducting market research for your own business, you would need to increase this number significantly.

Follow the steps below in preparing your written survey. Be sure to survey individuals in your target market (those to whom you plan to sell).

Step 1 – Revise Survey. Based on the feedback you received on your oral survey, make the appropriate revisions and prepare a typed version of your survey that can be administered impersonally (by mail, Internet, handout). All questions should be clear, unambiguous, and objective. Limit your survey to one page. Test your survey before distributing it by asking several people to complete it and provide feedback on content, clarity, and format.

A sample survey is provided on page 129. This is provided only as an example and should NOT be given out—you will develop your own survey to distribute.

Step 2 – Administer Survey. Identify your target market. Mail, e-mail, or hand out surveys to this market. Remember, some people will not return or respond to your survey, so you will need to send out extras, just in case. Disseminate enough to ensure a minimum of 10 responses.

B. Compile and Compute Survey Results

For each survey question, <u>record responses on a blank survey form</u> and tally responses. Then answer the following questions <u>on a separate sheet of paper</u>:

a. Describe your target market.
b. Whom did you survey?
 c. How many surveys were given out, and how many surveys were completed?
d. What were the key findings revealed through the surveys?
e. What can you conclude, if anything, from your findings? Note: You administered a very small number of surveys, so preliminary conclusions would need to be validated through additional research.
f. How will your survey assist you in developing, marketing, and pricing your product or service?
g. What changes will you make to your product/service, price, or marketing as a result of this activity?

C. Refine Survey

What changes will you make to your survey instrument as a result of this activity?

Sample Survey - Do NOT distribute

Note: This survey assumes a consumer (rather than business) market for the example used—this book, *Opportunity Analysis, Business Ideas: Identification and Evaluation*

Checkmark appropriate answers

Description: *Opportunity Analysis* is a 150-page practical guide in workbook format designed to assist potential entrepreneurs in identifying and evaluating business ideas.

A. The *Opportunity Analysis* book includes basic information on opportunity recognition and evaluation, entrepreneurial stories and examples, activities and resource listings. Would you purchase this book? ___ Yes ___ No. If no, why not?

B. What recommendations do you have for marketing *Opportunity Analysis*? (How would you expect to find out about this type of book?)
___ Bookstore(s)   ___ Newspaper   ___ Magazine article
___ Direct mail   ___ Speaker presentations   ___ Other (specify)

C. Review the features of the *Opportunity Analysis* book listed in item "A" above. Which feature(s) are most important to you and why?

What other features you would like to see included?

D. What do you see as the greatest benefit of purchasing (using) this book?
___ Time savings (a guided approach to identifying and evaluating business ideas)
___ Convenience of being able to work through material at one's own pace
___ Information on how to identify and evaluate business ideas.
___ Other (specify) _____

E. The price of *Opportunity Analysis* will be approximately $40.00.
Would you buy at this price? ___ Yes ___ No
What is the **most** you would be willing to pay for this book? $_____

F. Circle correct answers

What is your age?	18 – 25	26 – 35	36 – 50	over 50
What is your income?	Less than $25,000	$26, 000-$75,000	$76,000 - $100,000	Over $100,000
What is your education?	High school	Some college	College degree	Graduate degree

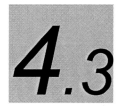

4.3

activity
competitive scan

For your No. 1 idea, look at the marketplace and identify businesses that offer the same or similar products or services—not just direct competitors but indirect ones as well. Check the local Yellow Page directory (for businesses selling directly to consumers) or a business directory for business-to-business sales. A business directory can be found in most libraries. If your product or service will be marketed nationally or internationally, use the Internet or library resources to assist you in identifying similar businesses.

List both direct and indirect competitors. If a business is a local establishment, a personal visit to the business will be the most effective method of obtaining information.

Business Name	Location	Products/Services	Strengths and Weaknesses
1.			
2.			

Business Name	Location	Products/Services	Strengths and Weaknesses
3.			
4.			
5.			

How will your business compare to the businesses listed? What is your competitive advantage?

4.4

activity
environmental scan

It is important to learn about the industry in which you will be operating. Trade associations can do a great deal to jumpstart your learning curve. A library visit or Internet search will yield SIC or NAIC codes and the names of relevant trade associations and journals.

A. **Identify the type of business you wish to start.**

B. **Identify your SIC or NAIC code.**

C. **Identify relevant industry information.**
   a. What local and/or national trade associations are related to your business idea?

   b. What professional journal(s) is (are) related to your business idea?

   c. Industry life cycle. Based on your knowledge of the industry in which you will be operating, is the industry in the introductory, growth, maturity, or decline stage? What data supports this?

d. Based on your industry life cycle assessment, what will be your most significant challenges?

D. Identify relevant factors in the macro environment.

Identify any macro-environmental changes that may affect your business. Consider regulatory, industry, technological, social, economic, and demographic changes. Include the source and date of information cited.

E. Identify relevant factors in the micro environment.

Identify relevant micro-environmental changes that may affect your particular trade area. Consider factors in the regulatory environment, economic and population changes, and the competitive environment. Include the source and date of information cited.

Getting Started

Before determining where to go from here, first consider where you have been.

Idea Identification—Steps 1 and 2

To come up with new business idea(s) or add to the ones you already have.

STEP 1 – Looking Inside	STEP 2 – Looking Outside
You → Work experiences Hobbies/interests Education/training	→ Chance discovery Personal network: Family & friends Suggestions from others Other sources: Creativity, trends, emulate, critique

---

Idea Evaluation—Steps 3 and 4

To evaluate your business ideas and identify the one that fits you best.

STEP 3 - Screening	STEP 4 – Further Investigation and Getting Started	The Key
Skills & talents	Concept testing	
Dreams & goals	Environmental screening	
Personal finances	Competitive scan	
Market viability	Customer identification	The Right Idea

Diagram 4.1

You've done a thorough job of coming up with ideas for businesses. You've pared your many ideas down to one or a manageable few. You've examined your strengths and talents and identified which ideas are the best match for you. You've begun your investigation of the marketplace and looked at your financial requirements and funding capabilities. You've conducted some very basic market research to test your idea and gain information about the marketplace. The work you have done throughout the book has greatly increased the odds that the business you are considering is the key to your entrepreneurial future.

CUSTOMER IDENTIFICATION

Now you're ready to move forward and take additional steps toward your goal. One important first step, to move from planning to action, is to identify potential first customers. Starting a business with customers ready to buy is the ideal way to begin. Entrepreneurs often procrastinate about contacting potential customers out of fear, inexperience, or lack of clarity on how to reach them. Clearly identifying early customers is critical to successfully launching your business. Within your target market, which you identified earlier, which customer(s) will you approach first?

In selecting your first or early customers, consider factors such as which ones will most likely buy? Be the easiest to reach? Be most receptive to a new vendor? Are influential with other potential buyers?

Your first or early customers can help you establish credibility and, in some cases, open doors for sales to new buyers. Sometimes they can act as advocates for your business, providing support and taking pride in your success. Are there customers who are highly respected by others in the industry or community that would be an asset to launching your business? Spend time thinking strategically about who these customers might be.

NETWORKING

Start networking now, even if your business start-up is planned for years down the road. You will access your network to find buyers, partners, investors, employees, vendors, contract workers, and so on. The first time you talk with someone is NOT the time to ask them to invest in your business or loan you money. Relationships take time to build.

Identifying a mentor can also be an important next step on your entrepreneurial journey. Most successful entrepreneurs identify one or a series of mentors who have guided them along the way. Consider who can fulfill this role in your life. Such individuals may be other entrepreneurs, professors, or business people such as bankers or suppliers.

Other entrepreneurs offering products similar to yours may also be a rich source of hands-on information. As long as you do not plan to compete with them in the same trade area, many are very willing to share their experience and knowledge. These "competitors at a distance" can be located using the Yellow Pages, Internet, or talking with others in the marketplace or industry. Later in this section, you will be directed to interview a "competitor at a distance." In addition to obtaining helpful information, this interview may also be the beginning of a rewarding or possibly mentoring relationship.

BUSINESS PLAN

As a follow up to the work you completed in this book, it is recommended that you develop a business plan for any business concept you are seriously considering. The business plan will help you continue the evaluation of the advisability of acting on your idea. A list of resources at the end of this section will help you gather additional information and examine areas previously touched upon, such as marketing and finance, in greater depth.

Keep in mind that it is not necessarily the great idea that succeeds. It is more likely the excellent implementation and execution of a worthwhile idea that will lead to your entrepreneurial success

Terms such as "the quantum leap" or "taking the plunge" have been used to describe the jumping off point of going from thinking and planning to actually doing—starting your own business. Millions of others have done so, believing the rewards far outweigh the risks. As Mark Towers, a guest columnist for *The Kansas City Star*, commented, "You don't necessarily think yourself into a new way of acting, but rather act yourself into a new way of thinking."

"Believe in yourself! Have faith in your abilities!
without a humble but reasonable confidence in your own
powers you cannot be successful or happy."

Norman Vincent Peale

What you have already done by completing the work in this book is to take a giant step toward launching your own business.

"when you come to a fork in the road, take it."

Yogi Berra

Congratulations!

4.5 activity
the Key
the business opportunity that is right for you

Summarize the following points related to your business concept.

a. Describe your business concept in detail.

b. What marketplace opportunity does your concept address?

c. How does this business concept match your skills and talents?

d. Who are your targeted customers and how will these customers be reached?

e. What is your next step — where do you go from here?

f. The step identified in "e" above will be completed by what date? _____

4.6 activity customer identification

a. Identify your first or early customers.

Who are they?	Where are they?	How can they be reached? *Networking, advertising, direct sales, distribution channels, other*
1._____	_____	_____
2._____	_____	_____
3._____	_____	_____

b. Identify the specific steps you will take to make your first sale.

c. The actions listed in "b" above will be completed by what date? _____

 **4.7**

activity
networking – competitor at
a distance

By talking to others, searching the Yellow Pages or Internet, or reading publications and news articles, identify a business similar to the one you wish to start but outside your trade area. Contact the entrepreneur and conduct an interview via personal visit or telephone. *Note: This may be the beginning of a mentoring relationship.*

Name of Entrepreneur _____

Name of Business _____ Phone _____

Address of Business _____

_____

_____E-mail _____

Number of Employees _____   Years in Business _____

Description of Product or Service _____

_____

_____

Possible Questions: To develop a questionnaire, choose relevant questions from the list below or develop your own.

a. What were (are) your main challenges in starting and growing the business?

b. What activities have been most effective in marketing your products?

c. What vendors/suppliers would you recommend?

d. What trade or professional associations have been helpful to you?

e. What financing sources have been helpful?

f. How do you price your product or service?

g. How have your products or services changed since you started and why?

h. Who is your target market? How did you identify it? Describe your typical customer.

i. Is your industry in the introduction, growth, maturity, or decline stage?

j. Approximately how much money was required to launch your business?

k. If you were to start over today, what would you do differently?

l. May I contact you in the future for additional information?

Resources

The following resources are a sample of what is available over the Internet or at your local library. A reference librarian at the library can assist you in finding these resources. A Library of Congress system, which is commonly used in college libraries, was used to identify references.

Reference Books for Starting a Business

The Business Plan Handbook REF HD62.7.B865. A multi-volume set that includes actual business plans developed by entrepreneurs seeking funding.

Small Business Profiles: A Guide to Today's Top Opportunities for Entrepreneurs REF HD62.7.S621. Covers important information for business start-up, such as costs, expected profits, financing, marketing, and obtaining licenses.

Small Business Sourcebook REF HD2346.U5S66. Lists resources that are important to more than 300 types of small businesses, including start-up information, franchises, trade associations, and trade magazines.

SBA Loans: A Step-By-Step Guide REF HG4027.7.O43. Covers the preparation of SBA loan requests, including loan application forms.

Identifying Customers

Household Spending: Who Spends How Much on What REF HC110.C6 H68
The American Marketplace: Demographics and Spending Patterns REF HA214 .A6
American Generations: Who They Are, How They Live, What They Think REF HC110.C6M545

Locating Demographic and Economic Information

Area chambers of commerce frequently provide information on local growth, traffic patterns, and economic trends.

Rand McNally. Commercial Atlas & Marketing Guide REF G1200.R3. Includes maps, retail sales, business conditions, buying power, transportation routes, etc.

The Sourcebook of ZIP Code Demographics REF HA 203.S66. Reports population counts by ZIP code and provides indexes of spending potential in different consumer categories for each ZIP code.

Statistical Abstract of the United States REF HA202.A5. U.S. industrial, social, political, and economic statistics.

Survey of Buying Power & Survey of Media Markets (Periodical). Annual "special" issue of *Sales & Marketing Management* magazine provides data related to buying power and retail sales.

Finding Information about local and regional companies

D & B Regional Business Directory. Covers specific metropolitan areas, including information on sales, business addresses, number of employees, line of business, etc.

Sorkins' Directory of Business & Government. Covers metropolitan areas, businesses, organizations, and government. Includes company name, executive name, key personnel, kind of business, indication of size by number of employees, and sales range.

Locating Industry Information

Encyclopedia of Trade Associations. Identifies trade associations, contact information, trade publications.

Key Business Ratios, One Year REF HF5681.B2 R25. Offers performance indicators for companies represented by about 800 SIC codes.

North American Industry Classification System 1997 REF HF1041.5.N674. Identifies NAIC codes, which are frequently used to research industry information.

RMA Annual Statement Studies REF HF5681.B2 R6. Covers 300 lines of business, including composite financial statements of companies, presented by SIC code.

Standard Industrial Classification Manual REF HF1042.A55. Identifies SIC codes, which are frequently used to research industry information.

U.S. Industry & Trade Outlook REF HC101.U54. Covers major industries, including historical data and one- and five-year forecasts.

Library Databases/Indexes

ABI/INFORM. Includes reporting and analysis of consumer attitudes, expenditures, marketing, and industry trends.

Business & Company Resource Center. Database to research topics on business and management. Includes information on consumer behavior and expenditures.

Lexis-Nexis Academic. Includes many full-text business periodicals and reports relevant to advertising/marketing.

Readers Guide to Periodical Literature. Provides indexing and accurate bibliographic data for over 272 popular magazines.

Trends

Dictionary of the Future—The Words, Terms and Trends that Define the Way We Live, Work and Talk by Faith Popcorn, Adam Hanft, © 2001.

Demographics of the US, Trends and Projections by Cheryl Russell, © 2000.

Future Survey, a monthly abstract of books, articles, forecasts, and trends, published by the World Future Society.

Global Trends 2005, An Owners Manual for the Next Decade by Michael J. Mazarr, © 2005.

It Takes a Prophet to Make a Profit: 15 Trends That Are Reshaping American Business by C. Britt Beemer and Robert L. Shook, © 2001.

The 100 Best Trends, 2006: Emerging Developments You Can't Afford to Ignore by George Ochoa and Melinda Corey, © 2005.

Think Forward, Get Ahead, and Cash in on the Future, Richard Laermer, © 2002.

Triumph of the Mundane: The Unseen Trends That Shape Our Lives and Environment by Hal Kane, © 2000.

Web sites

www.bizstats.com. Financial ratios, business statistics and benchmarks, online analysis of businesses and industries

www.bplans.com. Sample business plans and articles on business planning.

www.census.gov. U.S. Bureau of the Census. Comprehensive collection of social, demographic, and economic information.

www.census.gov/epcd/www/naics.html. North American Industry Classification System replaces SIC code.

www.edgar company search. The Securities and Exchange Commission's Electronic Data Gathering Analysis and Retrieval system, includes information on initial public offerings (IPOs) and 10-K reports, which highlights recent company activities and plans.

www.entrepreneur.com. Web site of *Entrepreneur* magazine, providing how-to guides and information on financial management, business plans, etc.

www.eventuring.org. An entrepreneur's guide to growth, sponsored by the Ewing Marion Kauffman Foundation.

www.FreeDemographics.com. 2000 Census Data, All Geographies and Radius Reports.

www.inc.com. Information offered by the editors of *Inc* magazine on writing a business plan, starting a business, etc.

www.osha.gov/oshstats/sicser.html. Enter industry name or SIC code number.

www.sba.gov/starting/indexbusplans.html. The Business Plan—Road Map to Success. This is a tutorial and self-paced activity provided by the SBA.

www.toolkit.cch.com. CCH Business Owner's Toolkit, A how-to for small business

www.trendwatching.com. Consumer trends.

www.urban.org. Information on demographic, social, and economic trends

Bibliography and Suggested Readings

Bhidē, Amar, *Origin and Evolution of New Businesses*, © 2000, Oxford University Press.

Carter, Nancy, Larry Cox, Paul Reynolds, William Gartner, Patricia Greene, and the Ewing Marion Kauffman Foundation, *The Entrepreneur Next Door*, © 2002.

Frank, Carol, *Do As I Say Not As I Did: Gaining Wisdom in Business Through the Mistakes of Highly Successful People.* © 2005. Dallas, TX: Brown Books Publishing Group.

Kourilsky, Marilyn, *Making a Job: A Basic Guide to Entrepreneurship Readiness*, © 1999, Ewing Marion Kauffman Foundation.

Longenecker, Justin, Carlos Moore, J. William Petty, *Small Business Management: an Entrepreneurial Emphasis*, © 2000, South-Western College Publishing.

Moltz, Barry J., *You Need to be a Little Crazy: The Truth About Starting and Growing Your Business*, © 2003, Dearborn Trade Publishing.

Planning & Growing a Business Venture, © 2001, Kauffman Center for Entrepreneurial Leadership at the Ewing Marion Kauffman Foundation.

Pride, William M., and O. C. Ferrell, *Marketing*, © 2000, Houghton Mifflin Company.

Wheeler, Jim, *The Power of Innovative Thinking—Let New Ideas Lead to Your Success*, © 1998.

Smilor, Ray, *Daring Visionaries: How Entrepreneurs Build Companies, Inspire Allegiance, and Create Wealth*, © 2001, Halbrook, MA: Adams Media Corporation.